D1300292

HANS MAGNUS ENZENSBERGER
SELECTED POEMS

HANS MAGNUS ENZENSBERGER

SELECTED POEMS

TRANSLATED BY

HANS MAGNUS ENZENSBERGER
MICHAEL HAMBURGER
AND
RITA DOVE & FRED VIEBAHN

THE SHEEP MEADOW PRESS
RIVERDALE-ON-HUDSON, NEW YORK

To the noble coolies of poetry,
translators in East and West,
with gratitude.

Designed and typeset by Sheep Meadow Press, PO Box 1345,
Riverdale-on-Hudson, NY 10471

Distributed by University Press of New England, 23 Main Street,
Hanover, NH 03755

Printed on acid-free paper in the United States. This book meets the
guidelines for permanence and durability of the Committee on
Production Guidelines for Book Longevity of the Council on Library
Resources.

Library of Congress Cataloging-in-Publication Data:

Enzensberger, Hans Magnus.
Selected poems: bilingual edition
    p.   cm.
  ISBN 1-878818-73-2 (acid-free. paper)
  1. Enzensberger, Hans Magnus Translations into English.
  I. Hamburger, Michael. II. Title.
  PT2609.N9A6 1999
  831' .914--dc21   99-14951
           CIP

The Sheep Meadow Press gratefully acknowledges the Bronx Council
on the Arts for their support.

INHALT

CONTENTS

KIOSK (1997)

Kiosk (1997)

INTRODUCTION

In one way or another, as a poet, polemicist and commentator, Hans Magnus Enzensberger has been not only present, but conspicuous in the English-language countries for nearly twenty-five years, so that it seems unnecessary and impertinent to introduce him here. On the strength of his own brilliant English version of his major poem *The Sinking of the Titanic* alone, he could even qualify as an English-language poet. Since, for most of the time, he has also been an outstandingly public poet, far less concerned with his inner life than with matters he could assume to be immediately recognisable as common property, a biographical summary would be largely irrelevant and unhelpful. As for his public activities and involvements, the most condensed account of them would call for book-length treatment; and so would a key to his range of reference and allusion in the poems, of the kind he himself appended to his 'Summer Poem' and is best qualified to provide.

No Introduction was included in the first book selection of Enzensberger's poems, published in Britain and America in 1968, nor in the Northern House pamphlet that preceded it by two years. Characteristically Enzensberger's own title for the 1968 book was *poems for people who don't read poems*. An Introduction was added to the Penguin paperback edition of the same year, with the neutral and less provocative title *Selected Poems*.

Since that time Enzensberger has given up the lower case style he chose for the title of the book, as for its contents; and the provocative stance he had taken up in his first German collection of 1957, called *the wolves defended against the lambs*. His experience not only as a poet but as an editor, publisher, journalist, anthologist and translator of other people's poems in languages that range from Spanish to Norwegian, will have taught him that it matters very little what readers a poet has in mind for his poems – or did before advertising techniques became as dominant as they have become even in the arts. *poems for people who don't read poems* was read by the relatively small number of people who read poems. The prose books – as provocative and polemical as the early poems – that were to follow fairly regularly since 1962 may have been read by a rather larger number of people, though they came out of the same concerns. If so, it was for the obvious reason that the reading of poems, not excluding anti-poems, is a habit and skill less widespread than the reading of prose, a medium shared with newspapers and the information industry.

From the first, Enzensberger's special function as a poet and prose writer arose from his awareness of being a West German just old enough to have received his early conditioning in the Third Reich, though he was only fifteen years old when it collapsed. Unlike many of his seniors and coevals, he was not content to blame the 'wolves' of an older generation for what that order had perpetrated. If he was to be the conscience of his own generation, as he was widely acknowledged to be in the sixties and seventies, he had to break with the conformism and the 'inwardness' – the moral alibi of so many of his predecessors – that had allowed the German 'lambs' to feel good while going to the slaughter, their own as well as that of those classified as goats. As recently as in his latest prose book, *Aussichten auf den Bürgerkrieg* (Prospects for Civil War) of 1993, Enzensberger insisted that the meekness of the lambs was and remains a prerequisite for every atrocity committed by the wolves. The peculiar tough-mindedness of his stance, always combined with the utmost elegance, is inseparable from that early recognition.

By tough-mindedness here I don't mean aggressiveness, though the incisive, abrasive rhetoric of his earliest poems was felt to be aggressive by many of his German readers. What I mean is that, in his compassion as much as in his quarrels with others, he has avoided appeals to emotions not tested by knowledge and intelligence; and the assumption, constant in his poems, that the survival of individuals, groups, nations and species has long ceased to be guaranteed, and can be achieved only if its defenders are as active, resourceful and resilient as those who endanger it.

As early as 1960, too, when he published a pioneering anthology of international modern poetry, he was prescient enough to call it a 'museum' – long before the term 'postmodernist' had gone into general – and dubious – circulation; and he explained why he considered modernism to be defunct in an essay included in his book *Einzelheiten* of 1962. What he renounced for himself – without disparaging its achievements – was the deliberate experimentation of former 'avantgardes' – and the very notion of progress in the arts implied by the word itself. This did not absolve him from the need to write well; and, when his themes demanded it, he made use of modernist devices like the 'collage' or 'montage' structure of longer poems, from 'Lachesis Lapponica' and 'Summer Poem' onwards. Where such poems are difficult or demanding, it is because Enzensberger knows things most of his readers do not know, put in not for the sake of innovation or idiosyncrasy but because in our time even public and moral issues cannot be adequately responded to in poetry without an awareness of their inherent complexities and contradictions. Whatever his themes – and Enzensberger's concerns were ecological, as well as social and political, almost from the start – Enzensberger has grappled with those complexities and contradictions, to the point of giving up poetry itself for a while, as a medium no longer capable of serving the cause of survival. That was at a time when West German literature had been politicised and ideologised to an extent that tended to make the personal decisions of an established writer exemplary and prescriptive, quite especially if he was a writer in the thick of all the controversies, as Enzensberger was at the time, not only as a poet but as the editor of the radical periodical *Kursbuch* (Railway Timetable!). This crisis and dilemma had to be overcome by distinguishing what had looked like a strictly political commitment from the moral commitment much more compatible with good imaginative writing, whether in prose or verse. The turningpoint came with Enzensberger's stay in Cuba in 1969, during which he began work on *The Sinking of The Titanic*, first published in Germany in 1978. His Cuban experiences were woven into the broken narrative of that poem, together with many other layers, seeming interpolations, digressions, leaps in space, time and even manner.

Enzensberger's modernity – as distinct from modernism – lies in his exceptional grasp of the pluralism of our age. His work embodies the multiple awareness with which all of us are cursed by the sheer quantity and instant transmission of information, disaster, scandal, sensation, selected news of the world. It has been Enzensberger's distinction not to have recoiled from this battery of appeals to our interest, sympathy, anger and outrage, but to have gone out of his way to be more widely informed than most of the more specialised transmitters – about science and technology as much as the most diverse societies, their economics and politics, not to mention linguistics, history and the arts. At one time, I remember, he went so far as to purge his library of 'belles lettres', in favour of reference books, manuals, treatises and factual reports. He was so shocked to find that I made do with a long superseded printing of the Concise Oxford English Dictionary that he gave me a copy of the Shorter Oxford English Dictionary, still in use, with the inscription: 'eine hand voll wort-futter für die vögel in michaels kopf' – 'a handful of word-feed for the bats in Michael's belfry.' If the bats in my belfry were only fattened by that food, the likelihood of that outcome was implicit in the inscription. Radical though he used to be, Enzensberger has never been simplistic.

This Sheep Meadow Press selection includes all the poems

translated by Enzensberger himself or by me for the early pamphlet and books, together with our uncollected later translations and his own extracts from his book-length poem. His latest German collection, *Zukunfts-musik* (1991) is so different from his earlier work that it does seem to call for something in the way of introduction, if only because it may be felt to contradict the little I have written here about his work in general.

Lateness, in fact, marks not only the manner but the themes of these poems; and the change is as much a personal one, a sense of one man's time running out, as a political and cultural one, since in his poems Enzensberger has always merged personal concerns in general ones. Several of the poems in the first section of the book have to do with paintings and painters, all the poems in the book with ways of looking. Enzensberger's increasingly historical perspective on art links up with earlier work in his book of prose poems Mausoleum of 1975 and in the collection Die Furie des Verschwindens (The Fury of Disappearance) of 1980, much as the second section links up with the sociological preoccupations that were prominent in his work from the start.

What has changed is Enzensberger's stance. The same poet who could once claim to write poems for people who don't read poems will be neither understood or appreciated now by any reader whose mind and ear are not receptive to the most delicate modulations of the medium; and even such readers could find Enzensberger's late manner deficient in immediacy and the sensuousness which Milton thought essential to the language of poetry. It isn't only that the new poems are less direct and unambiguous. The difficulty – for English readers especially, with their preference for identifiable particulars of situation, scene or person, for referential images – has to do with a degree of abstraction that some will think more suitable in the visual arts and music than in poetry.

In Enzensberger's recent prose books, too, his stance has changed from one of mundane and differentiated partiality to one of amused, benign and impartial detachment. In the late poems his scepticism extends to the diction as much as to the message; and his wit has ceased to be a weapon with a single edge. The precision of the late poems is due less to a command of language and idiom, to his old eloquence, than to a questioning of them. The character studies still prominent in *Die Furie Des Verschwindens*, too, have given way to an intense questioning of what and how we speak, what and how we perceive. Though the same material is drawn upon – the wide experience and interests of a lifetime – it is presented much more hesitantly, probingly and searchingly, without the early Enzensberger's assurance of a representative function. The social and moral criticism of the earlier books of poems has become existential, almost metaphysical in places.

Ageing itself may have a good deal to do with the change. The ironic title of the book – *Music of the Future* – is a more telling pointer, because both past and future are more operative in these poems than Enzensberger's earlier responses to topical issues; and no contemplation of the future now is conducive to the certainties that has sustained his polemics in verse and prose. The title poem, the last in the book and not among those we had translated, evokes a music of the future that is more like a silence:

> That which we can't wait for
> will show us.
> It gleams, is uncertain, remote.
>
> That which we let come towards us,
> does not await us,
> does not come towards us,
> does not come back to us,
> stands off.
>
> Does not belong to us,
> does not enquire about us,
> doesn't want to know about us,
> tells us nothing,
> is not our due.
>
> Was not,
> is not there for us,
> has never been there,
> is never there,
> is never.

This is a poetry less of enactment than of evaluation, and a poetry of bare bones. The few adjectives in it carry more weight than adjectives usually do in poems; and these adjectives take on a character more metaphorical than descriptive or decorative. Once again it is a rare advantage to English-speaking readers that Enzensberger was able and willing to contribute his own versions of poems so bare as to be barely translatable.

MICHAEL HAMBURGER

*Enzensberger had not yet published *Kiosk* when Mr. Hamburger wrote this essay.

LANGUAGE OF THE COUNTRY
LANDESSPRACHE

(1960)

Landessprache

Ostendebat namque varium iracundum iniustum
inconstantem eundem exorabilem clementem
misericordem gloriosum excelsum humilem
ferocem fugacemque et omnia pariter.
PLINIUS, Hist. nat. XXXV, XXXVI.

Was habe ich hier verloren,
in diesem Land,
dahin mich gebracht haben meine Älteren
durch Arglosigkeit?
Eingeboren, doch ungetrost,
abwesend bin ich hier,
ansässig im gemütlichen Elend,
in der netten, zufriedenen Grube.

Was habe ich hier? und was habe ich hier zu suchen,
in dieser Schlachtschüssel, diesem Schlaraffenland,
wo es aufwärts geht, aber nicht vorwärts,
wo der Überdruß ins bestickte Hungertuch beißt,
wo in den Delikateßgeschäften die Armut, kreidebleich,
mit erstickter Stimme aus dem Schlagrahm röchelt und ruft:
es geht aufwärts!
wo eine Gewinnspanne weit von den armen Reichen die reichen Armen
vor Begeisterung ihre Kinostühle zerschmettern,
da geht es aufwärts von Fall zu Fall,
wo die Zahlungsbilanz Hosianna und alles was recht ist singt
und ruft: das ist nicht genug,
daß da die Freizeit spurt und Gas gibt und hinhaut,
das ist das kleinere Übel, das ist nur die Hälfte,
das macht nichts, das ist nicht genug,
daß die Tarifpartner durch die Straßen irren
und mit geballten Fäusten frohlocken
und singen und sagen:

hier geht es aufwärts,
hier ist gut sein,
wo es rückwärts aufwärts geht,
hier schießt der leitende Herr den leitenden Herrn mit dem Gesangbuch ab,
hier führen die Leichtbeschädigten mit den Schwerbeschädigten Krieg,

Language of the Country

He displayed them as fickle, choleric, unjust
and variable, but also placable and merciful
and compassionate, boastful, lofty and humble,
fierce and timid — and all these at the same time.
PLINY, Natural History XXXV, XXXVI.

What am I doing here,
in this country
to which my elders brought me
intending no harm?
Native but comfortless
absently I am here,
settled in cosy squalor,
in this nice, contented hole.

What do I have here? What business
in this bean feast, this never-never-land
where things are looking up but getting nowhere,
where surfeited hunger chews the embroidered napkin,
where in delicatessen shops poverty, white as chalk,
with stifled voice gasps through whipped cream, and calls out
things are looking up!
Where a profit margin away from the poor rich the rich poor
smash their cinema seats for sheer joy
because things are looking up, more so every day,
where the balance of payments and fair enough sing
and call out: it is not enough
that leisure booms and steps on the gas and gets going,
this is the lesser evil, this is only one half,
this makes no difference, this is not enough,
that the wage negotiators wander lost in the streets
and with clenched fists rejoice
and sing and proclaim:

here things are looking up,
all's right with the world
where things are looking up backwards,
here hymnbooks decide what boss will be picked by the bosses,
here the partly disabled wage war against the wholly disabled,

hier heißt es unerbittlich nett zueinander sein,

und das ist das kleinere Übel,
das wundert mich nicht,
das nehmen die Käufer in Kauf,
hier, wo eine Hand die andere kauft,
Hand aufs Herz, hier sind wir zuhaus,

hier laßt uns Hütten bauen,
auf diesem arischen Schrotthaufen,
auf diesem krächzenden Parkplatz,
wo aus den Ruinen Ruinen sprossen,
nagelneu, Ruinen auf Vorrat, auf Raten,
auf Abruf, auf Widerruf:

Hiersein ist herrlich,
wo dem verbrauchten Verbraucher,
und das ist das kleinere Übel,
die Haare ausfallen,
wo er sein erfolgreiches Haupt verhüllt
mit Wellpappe und Cellophan,
wo er abwesend aus der Grube ruft:
hier laßt uns Hütten bauen,

in dieser Mördergrube,
wo der Kalender sich selber abreißt vor Ohnmacht und Hast,
wo die Vergangenheit in den Müllschluckern schwelt
und die Zukunft mit falschen Zähnen knirscht,
das kommt davon, daß es aufwärts geht,
da tun wir Fleckenwasser drauf,
das ist hier so üblich, das wundert mich nicht,

goldrichtig liegen wir hier,
wo das Positive zum Höchstkurs notiert,
die Handelskammern decken sich damit ein
und bahren es auf unter Panzerglas,

wo wir uns finden wohl unter Blinden,
in den Schau-, Kauf- und Zeughäusern,
und das ist nicht alles, das ist nur die Hälfte,
das ist die tiefgefrorene Wildnis,
das ist die erfolgreiche Raserei, das tanzt

4

here the rule is: be ruthlessly nice to each other,

and this is the lesser evil,
this does not surprise me,
this the bargainers bargain with,
here, where one hand buys the other,
cross my heart, shake hands, here we're at home,

here let us build tabernacles,
on this Ayran dump of scrap,
where from ruins ruins sprout
brand new, ruins in stock,
ruins by standing order,
by instalments, sale or return:

To be here is glorious, — *parody of Rilke*
where the consumptive consumer,
and this is the lesser evil,
loses his hair,
where he hides his successful head
under cardboard and plastic bags,
where absently he calls out from the hole:
here let us build tabernacles

in this murderer's den
where in haste and impotence the calendar tears its own leaves,
where the past rots and reeks in the rubbish disposal unit
and the future grits its false teeth,
that's all because things are looking up,
we treat it with stain removers,
that's our custom here, this does not surprise me,

right as gold we lie here
where positive values are quoted at peak prices,
the chambers of commerce lay in stock
and lay it out in state under bulletproof glass,

where on the bonny bonny banks we play blind man's buff,
in exhibition rooms, arsenals, sale rooms,
and this is not all, this is only one half,
this is the frozen-up waste,
this is successful madness, this dances

im notdürftigen Nerz, auf zerbrochenen Knien,
im ewigen Frühling der Amnesie,
das ist ein anderes Land als andere Länder,
das reut mich, und daß es mich reut,
das ist das kleinere Übel, denn das ist wahr,
was seine Opfer, ganz gewöhnliche tote Leute,
aus der Erde rufen, etwas Laut- und Erfolgloses,
das an das schalldichte Pflaster dringt
von unten, und es beschlägt, daß es dunkel wird,
fleckig, naß, bis eine Lache,
eine ganz gewöhnliche Lache es überschwemmt,

und den Butzemann überschwemmt,
das Löweneckerchen, das Allerleirauh,
und die schöne Rapunzel, die sind nicht mehr hier,
und es gibt keine Städte mehr, und keine Fische,
die sind erstickt in dieser Lache,

wie meine Brüder, die tadel- und hilflosen Pendler,
wie sie mich reuen, die frommen Gerichtsvollzieher,
die Gasmänner, wie sie waten zuhauf,
mit ihren Plombierzangen, wie sie stapfen,
mit ihren abwesenden Stiefeln, durchs Bodenlose,
die Gloriole vorschriftsmäßig tief im Genick:

ja wären's Leute wie andere Leute,
war es ein ganz gewöhnliches, ein andres
als dieses Nacht- und Nebelland,
von Abwesenden überfüllt,
die wer sie sind nicht wissen noch wissen wollen,
die in dieses Land geraten sind
auf der Flucht vor diesem Land
und werden flüchtig sein bis zur Grube:

wärs anders, wär ihm zu helfen,
wäre Rat und Genugtuung hier,
wär es nicht dieses brache, mundtote Feindesland!

Was habe ich hier verloren, was suche ich
und stochre in diesem unzuständigen Knäuel
von Nahkampfspangen, Genußscheinen,
Gamsbärten, Schlußverkäufen, und finde nichts

in needy mink, on broken knees,
in amnesia's eternal springtime,
this is a country different from any other,
this makes me remorseful, and this remorse of mine
is the lesser evil, for this is the truth
which its victims, people quite ordinary and dead,
call out from under the earth, something soundless and unsuccessful,
something that beats against the soundproof pavement
from down below and dims it, so it grows dark,
spotty, wet, till a puddle,
a puddle quite ordinary spreads where it was,

and covers the fairy tale dwarf,
the larch tree, little grey mouse
and lovely Rapunzel, these are no longer here,
and there are no cities left, and no fishes,
these have choked in that puddle,

like my brothers, the blameless and helpless commuters,
how remorseful they make me, the pious bailiffs,
the gasmen, how they wade all together,
with their seals and pincers, how they stamp
in their absent boots, over the bottomless places,
their statutory haloes low on their necks:

all right, if these were people like any others,
if it were a quite ordinary country,
different from this land of night and mist
overcrowded with absent people
who neither know nor want to know who they are,
who have come to this country
on their flight from this country
and will be in flight till they're buried:

if it were different it could be helped,
there'd be comfort and satisfaction,
if it were not this fallow, silenced and hostile land.

What am I doing here, why do I try
to undo this incompetent tangle
of close combat bars, of bonus vouchers,
chamois beard hats, closing down sales, and find nothing

als chronische, chronologisch geordnete Turnhallen
und Sachbearbeiter für die Menschlichkeit
in den Kasernen für die Kasernen für die Kasernen:

Was soll ich hier? und was soll ich sagen?
in welcher Sprache? und wem?
Da tut mir die Wahl weh wie ein Messerstich,
das reut mich, das ist das kleinere Übel,
das schreit und so weiter
mit kleinen Schreien zum Himmel
und gibt sich für größer aus als es ist,
aber es ist nicht ganz,
es ist nur die himmelschreiende Hälfte,
es ist noch nicht genug:

denn dieses Land, vor Hunger rasend,
zerrauft sich sorgfältig mit eigenen Händen,
dieses Land ist von sich selber geschieden,
ein aufgetrenntes, inwendig geschiedenes Herz,
unsinnig tickend, eine Bombe aus Fleisch,
eine nasse, abwesende Wunde:

Deutschland, mein Land, unheilig Herz der Völker,
ziemlich verrufen, von Fall zu Fall,
unter allen gewöhnlichen Leuten:

Meine zwei Länder und ich, wir sind geschiedene Leute,
und doch bin ich inständig hier,
in Asche und Sack, und frage mich:
was habe ich hier verloren?

Das habe ich hier verloren,
was auf meiner Zunge schwebt,
etwas andres, das Ganze,
das furchtlos scherzt mit der ganzen Welt
und nicht in dieser Lache ertrinkt,

verloren an dieses fremde, geschiedne Geröchel,
das gepreßte Geröchel im *Neuen Deutschland*,
das Frankfurter Allgemeine Geröchel
(und das ist das kleinere Übel),
ein mundtotes Würgen, das nichts von sich weiß,

but chronic, chronologically graded gymnasiums
and specialists in charge of humanity
in barracks for barracks for barracks:

What's my purpose here? and what shall I say?
in what language? to whom?
this decision hurts like the stab of a knife,
this makes me remorseful, this is the lesser evil
this screams and so forth
with little screams up to heaven
and pretends to be bigger than it is,
but it is not the whole,
it is only one half crying out to heaven,
it still is not enough:

for this country, raving with hunger,
carefully tears itself to pieces with its own hands,
this country is divided from itself,
a rent, an inwardly divided heart
senselessly ticking, a bomb made of flesh,
a wet, an absent wound:

Germany, my country, unholy heart of the nations,
pretty notorious, more so every day,
among ordinary people elsewhere:

my two countries and I, we've gone separate ways,
and yet I am wholly here
in sackcloth and ashes, and ask:
what is my business here?

My business here is with that
which hovers on my tongue,
something different, the whole,
that fearlessly, gaily consorts with the whole world
and does not drown in the puddle,

lost to this alien divided gasping,
the stifled gasping in our *New Germany,*
the *Frankfurter Allgemeine* gasping
(and this is the lesser evil)
a silenced groan that knows nothing about itself,

von dem ich nichts wissen will, Musterland,
Mördergrube, in die ich herzlich geworfen bin
bei halbwegs lebendigem Leib,
da bleibe ich jetzt,
ich hadere aber ich weiche nicht,
da bleibe ich eine Zeitlang,
bis ich von hinnen fahre zu den anderen Leuten,
und ruhe aus, in einem ganz gewöhnlichen Land,
hier nicht,
nicht hier.

about which I want to know nothing, model country,
murderer's den into which I've been heartily thrown
half living still, half alive,
there I am staying now,
I grumble but do not budge,
there I shall stay for a time,
till I move on to the other people
and rest, in a country quite ordinary,
elsewhere,
not here.

Das Ende der Eulen

Ich spreche von euerm nicht,
ich spreche vom Ende der Eulen.
Ich spreche von Butt und Wal
in ihrem dunkeln Haus,
dem siebenfältigen Meer,
von den Gletschern,
sie werden kalben zu früh,
Rab und Taube, gefiederten Zeugen,
von allem was lebt in Lüften
und Wäldern, und den Flechten im Kies,
vom Weglosen selbst, und vom grauen Moor
und den leeren Gebirgen:

Auf Radarschirmen leuchtend
zum letzten Mal, ausgewertet
auf Meldetischen, von Antennen
tödlich befingert Floridas Sümpfe
und das sibirische Eis, Tier
und Schilf und Schiefer erwürgt
von Warnketten, umzingelt
vom letzten Manöver, arglos
unter schwebenden Feuerglocken,
im Ticken des Ernstfalls.

Wir sind schon vergessen.
Sorgt euch nicht um die Waisen,
aus dem Sinn schlagt euch
die mündelsichern Gefühle,
den Ruhm, die rostfreien Psalmen.
Ich spreche nicht mehr von euch,
Planern der spurlosen Tat,
und von mir nicht, und keinem.
Ich spreche von dem was nicht spricht,
von den sprachlosen Zeugen,
von Ottern und Robben,
von den alten Eulen der Erde.

The End of Owls

I do not speak of what's yours,
I speak of the end of the owls.
I speak of turbot and whale
in their glimmering house,
in the sevenfold sea,
of the glaciers—
too soon they will calve—
raven and dove, the feathered witnesses,
of all that lives in the winds
and woods, and the lichen on rock,
of impassable tracts and the grey moors
and the empty mountain ranges:

Shining on radar screens
for the last time, recorded,
checked out on consoles, fingered
by aerials fatally Florida's marshes
and the Siberian ice, animal,
reed and slate all strangled
by interlinked warnings, encircled
by the last manoeuvres, guileless
under hovering cones of fire,
while the time-fuses tick.

As for us, we're forgotten.
Don't give a thought to the orphans,
expunge from your minds
your gilt-edged security feelings
and fame and the stainless psalms.
I don't speak of you any more,
planners of vanishing actions,
nor of me, nor of anyone.
I speak of that without speech,
of the unspeaking witnesses,
of otters and seals,
of the ancient owls of the earth.

Die Hebammen

In brausenden Trauben schwärmen sie aus,
wenn der Morgen graut, klettern
über Hecken und Brücken behend
und belagern die fernsten Gehöfte.

Ihre prallen glänzenden Koffer drohn
wie schwarze Bomben, glimmend
auf Gletschern und Bahnsteigen,
Mooren, Hopfenfeldern und Riffen.

Die Nüstern der Ammen blähn sich vor Gier:
Wo es nach heißen Handtüchern riecht,
springen sie unverhofft querfeldein,
drücken knurrend die Türen auf
und werfen sich über die Betten.

Sie reißen ein Fleisch zur Welt,
das wenig wiegt, ein weißes Fleisch,
das ein paar dutzendmal überwintert:
dann ist es hin, und sie zerren
ans Licht einen Zornschrei,
der, wenn es Mittag wird, schallt
durch die Steinbrüche und erstickt
in einem Gewölk bleicher Windeln.

Dann, gegen Abend, sieht sie der Mond
bei ihren blutigen Zangen und Nadeln
und Scheren kauern, lahm, im Moos,
wie schlaflose Raben, frösteln,
starren in den weglosen kahlen
Straßengraben der nahenden Nacht.

The Midwives

In buzzing clusters out they swarm
in the grey light of daybreak clamber
limberly over hedges and bridges
and lay siege to remotest homesteads.

Their taut and gleaming toolbags threaten
like black time-bombs, glimmering
on glaciers and railway platforms,
on moors and hopfields and sandbanks.

The midwives' nostrils distend with greed:
wherever it smells of hot towels
cross-country they skip unforeseen,
push open doors with a growl
and hurl themselves at the bedsteads.

Into the world they rip
flesh that weighs little, white flesh
that survives a few dozen winters:
then it's done for; they drag
to the light a furious roar
which, towards noon, rings out
through the quarries and fades away,
choked in a cloud of pale napkins.

Later the moon sees them crouch
over bloody forceps and nedles
and scissors, lame, in the moss
like sleepless ravens, chilly,
stare at the pathless blank
ditch of the oncoming night.

BRAILLE
BLINDENSCHRIFT

(1964)

Küchenzettel

An einem müßigen Nachmittag, heute
seh ich in meinem Haus
durch die offene Küchentür
eine Milchkanne   ein Zwiebelbrett
einen Katzenteller.
Auf dem Tisch liegt ein Telegramm.
Ich habe es nicht gelesen.

In einem Museum zu Amsterdam
sah ich auf einem alten Bild
durch die offene Küchentür
eine Milchkanne   einen Brotkorb
einen Katzenteller.
Auf dem Tisch lag ein Brief.
Ich habe ihn nicht gelesen.

In einem Sommerhaus an der Moskwa
sah ich vor wenig Wochen
durch die offene Küchentür
einen Brotkorb   ein Zwiebelbrett
einen Katzenteller.
Auf dem Tisch lag die Zeitung.
Ich habe sie nicht gelesen.

Durch die offene Küchentür
seh ich vergossene Milch
Dreißigjährige Kriege
Tränen auf Zwiebelbrettern
Anti-Raketen-Raketen
Brotkörbe
Klassenkämpfe.

Links unten ganz in der Ecke
seh ich einen Katzenteller.

Bill of Fare

One idle afternoon, today
in my house I see
through the open kitchen door
a milk jug   a chopping board
a plate for the cat.
A telegram lies on the table
I have not read it.

In a museum at Amsterdam
in an old picture I saw
through the open kitchen door
a milk jug   a bread basket
a plate for the cat.
A letter lay on the table.
I have not read it.

In a dacha on the Moskwa
a few weeks ago I saw
through the open kitchen door
a bread basket   a chopping board
a plate for the cat.
A newspaper lay on the table
I have not read it.

Through the open kitchen door
I see spilt milk
Thirty Years' wars
tears on chopping boards
anti-rocket rockets
bread baskets
class wars.

Low down in the left corner
I see a plate for the cat.

Abgelegenes Haus
(für Günter Eich)

Wenn ich erwache
schweigt das Haus.
Nur die Vögel lärmen.
Ich sehe aus dem Fenster
niemand. Hier

führt keine Straße vorbei.
Es ist kein Draht am Himmel
und kein Draht in der Erde.
Ruhig liegt das Lebendige
unter dem Beil.

Ich setze das Wasser auf.
Ich schneide mein Brot.
Unruhig drücke ich
auf den roten Knopf
des kleinen Transistors.

»Karibische Krise…wäscht weißer
und weißer und weißer…
einsatzbereit…Stufe drei…
That's the way I love you…
Montanwerte kräftig erholt…«

Ich nehme nicht das Beil.
Ich schlage das Gerät nicht in Stücke.
Die Stimme des Schreckens
beruhigt mich, sie sagt:
Wir sind noch am Leben.

Das Haus schweigt.
Ich weiß nicht, wie man Fallen stellt
und eine Axt macht aus Flintstein,
wenn die letzte Schneide
verrostet ist.

Remote House

(for Günter Eich)

When I wake up
the house is silent.
Only the birds make a noise.
Through the window I see
no one. Here

no road passes.
There is no wire in the sky
and no wire in the earth.
Quiet the living things lie
under the axe.

I put water on to boil.
I cut my bread.
Unquiet I press
the red push-button
of the small transistor.

'Caribbean crisis…washes whiter
and whiter and whiter…
troops ready to fly out…
phase three…*that's the way I love you*…
amalgamated steel stocks are back to par…'

I do not take the axe.
I do not smash the gadget to pieces.
The voice of terror
calms me; it says:
We are still alive.

The house is silent.
I do not know how to set traps
or make an axe out of flint,
when the last blade
has rusted.

Camera obscura

In meinen vier vorläufigen Wänden
aus Fichtenholz
vier mal fünf mal zweieinhalb Meter
in meinem winzigen Zimmer
bin ich allein

allein mit dem Bratapfel, der Dunkelheit,
der Sechzig-Watt-Birne,
mit der Bundeswehr, mit der Eule
allein

mit dem Briefbeschwerer aus blauem Glas,
der Kybernetik, dem Tod,
mit der Stuckrosette
allein

mit dem Gottseibeiuns
und dem Weiherweg in Kaufbeuren
(Reg. Bez. Schwaben)
mit meiner Milz allein

mit meinem Gevatter Rabmüller,
vor zwanzig Jahren vergast,
allein mit dem roten Telefon,
und mit vielem, was ich mir merken will.

Allein mit Krethi und Plethi,
Bouvard und Pécuchet,
Kegel und Kind,
Pontius und Pilatus.

In meinem unendlichen Zimmer
vier mal fünf mal zweieinhalb Meter
bin ich allein mit einem Spiralnebel
von Bildern

Camera Obscura

Within my four provisional walls
of firwood
twelve by twenty by seven feet
in my diminutive room
I am alone

alone with baked apples, the dark,
the sixty-watt bulb,
the federal army, the owl
alone

with the paperweight of blue glass,
with cybernetics, with death,
with the plaster rosette
alone

with Old Nick
and the pondside lane at Kaufbeuren
(Admin. Reg. Swabia)
alone with my spleen

with my godfather Rabmüller,
gassed twenty years ago,
alone with the red telephone
and with much that I want to remember.

Alone with Tom, Dick and Harry,
Bouvard and Pécuchet,
with kith and kin and chattels,
Pontius and Pilate.

In my infinite room
twelve by twelve by seven feet
I am alone with a spiral nebula
of images

von Bildern von Bildern
von Bildern von Bildern von Bildern
enzyklopädisch und leer
und unzweifelhaft

allein mit meinem vorläufigen Gehirn
darin ich wiederfinde den Bratapfel,
die Dunkelheit, den Gevatter Rabmüller,
und vieles was ich vergessen will.

of images of images
of images of images of images
encyclopaedic and empty
and not to be doubted

alone with my provisional brain
in which I discover baked apples,
the dark, my godfather Rabmüller
and much that I want to forget.

Ufer

Am andern Ufer, im grauen Morgen
entscheidet sich wer ich bin
in einem Rauch.

Ich rieche den Hanf hier, den Teer,
das verwitterte Holz.
Anderswo sind die andern.

Der Bootssteg zittert,
aber die Schritte
tragen nicht weit.

Es ist wenig zu sehen.

Draußen im Wasser treibt etwas,
etwas Bleiches treibt ab.
Rümpfe von Bäumen, von Kähnen,
von Männern.

Ruf nur, sage ich, ruf
mit deiner bleichen Stimme,
die Worte tragen nicht weit
in einem Rauch.

Am andern Ufer,
immer am andern Ufer
entscheidet sich was das ist:
dieser Hanf, dies Holz,
dieser verwitterte Schrei.

Gibt es ein anderes Ufer?

Nichts überhole ich.
Nichts holt mich über.
Nichts entscheidet sich hier.
Hier herrscht eine große Ruhe.

Es ist wenig zu sehen.

Langsam trocknet der Hanf
in einem Rauch.

Shore

On the other shore, in the grey morning
what I am is decided
in a haze of smoke.

I smell the hemp here, the tar,
the mouldering wood.
The others are elsewhere.

The landing-stage quivers
but my steps
do not take me far.

There isn't much one can see.

Out in the water something drifts.
Something pale drifts away.
Stumps of trees, of boats,
of men.

Cry out, then, I say.
Cry out with your pale voice.
The words will not go far
in a haze of smoke.

On the other shore,
always the other shore
what these are is decided:
this hemp, this wood,
this mouldering cry.

Is there another shore?

I overtake nothing.
Nothing takes me over.
Nothing is decided here.
Here a great stillness reigns.

There isn't much one can see.

Slowly the hemp dries
in a haze of smoke.

Der Andere

Einer lacht
kümmert sich
hält mein Gesicht mit Haut und Haar unter den Himmel
läßt Wörter rollen aus meinem Mund
einer der Geld und Angst und einen Paß hat
einer der streitet und liebt
einer rührt sich
einer zappelt

aber nicht ich
Ich bin der andere
der nicht lacht
der kein Gesicht unter dem Himmel hat
und keine Wörter in seinem Mund
der unbekannt ist mit sich und mit mir
nicht ich: der Andere: immer der Andere
der nicht siegt noch besiegt wird
der sich nicht kümmert
der sich nicht rührt

der Andere
der sich gleichgültig ist
von dem ich nicht weiß
von dem niemand weiß wer er ist
der mich nicht rührt
das bin ich

The Other

One laughs
is worried
under the sky exposes my face and my hair
makes words roll out of my mouth
one who has money and fears and a passport
one who quarrels and loves
one moves
one struggles

but not I
I am the other
who does not laugh
who has no face to expose to the sky
and no words in his mouth
who is unacquainted with me with himself
not I: the other: always the other
who neither wins nor loses
who is not worried
who does not move

the other
indifferent to himself
of whom I know nothing
of whom nobody knows who he is
who does not move me
that is I

Auf das Grab eines friedlichen Mannes

Dieser da war kein Menschenfreund,
mied Versammlungen, Kaufhäuser, Arenen.
Seinesgleichen Fleisch aß er nicht.

Auf den Straßen ging die Gewalt
lächelnd, nicht nackt.
Aber es waren Schreie am Himmel.

Die Gesichter der Leute waren nicht deutlich.
Sie schienen zertrümmert,
noch ehe der Schlag gefallen war.

Eines, um das er zeitlebens gekämpft hat,
mit Wörtern und Zähnen, ingrimmig,
hinterlistig, auf eigene Faust:

das Ding, das er seine Ruhe nannte
da er es hat, nun ist kein Mund mehr
an seinem Gebein, es zu schmecken.

For the Grave of a Peace-loving Man

This one was no philanthropist,
avoided meetings, stadiums, the large stores.
Did not eat the flesh of his own kind.

Violence walked the streets,
smiling, not naked.
But there were screams in the sky.

People's faces were not very clear.
They seemed to be battered
even before the blow had struck home.

One thing for which he fought all his life,
with words, tooth and claw, grimly,
cunningly, off his own bat:

the thing which he called his peace,
now that he's got it, there is no longer a mouth
over his bones, to taste it with.

Middle Class Blues

Wir können nicht klagen.
Wir haben zu tun.
Wir sind satt.
Wir essen.

Das Gras wächst,
das Sozialprodukt,
der Fingernagel,
die Vergangenheit.

Die Straßen sind leer.
Die Abschlüsse sind perfekt.
Die Sirenen schweigen.
Das geht vorüber.

Die Toten haben ihr Testament gemacht.
Der Regen hat nachgelassen.
Der Krieg ist noch nicht erklärt.
Das hat keine Eile.

Wir essen das Gras.
Wir essen das Sozialprodukt.
Wir essen die Fingernägel.
Wir essen die Vergangenheit.

Wir haben nichts zu verheimlichen.
Wir haben nichts zu versäumen.
Wir haben nichts zu sagen.
Wir haben.

Die Uhr ist aufgezogen.
Die Verhältnisse sind geordnet.
Die Teller sind abgespült.
Der letzte Autobus fährt vorbei.

Er ist leer.

Wir können nicht klagen.

Worauf warten wir noch?

Middle Class Blues

We can't complain.
We're not out of work.
We don't go hungry.
We eat.

The grass grows,
the social product,
the fingernail,
the past.

The streets are empty.
The deals are closed.
The sirens are silent.
All that will pass.

The dead have made their wills.
The rain's become a drizzle.
The war's not yet been declared.
There's no hurry for that.

We eat the grass.
We eat the social product.
We eat the fingernails.
We eat the past.

We have nothing to conceal.
We have nothing to miss.
We have have nothing to say.
We have.

The watch has been wound up.
The bills have been paid.
The washing-up has been done.
The last bus is passing by.

It is empty.

We can't complain.

What are we waiting for?

Bildnis eines Spitzels

Im Supermarkt lehnt er
unter der Plastiksonne,
die weißen Flecken in seinem Gesicht
sind Wut, nicht Schwindsucht,
hundert Schachteln Knuspi-Knackers
(*weil sie so herzhaft sind*)
zündet er mit den Augen an,
ein Stück Margarine
(die gleiche Marke wie ich:
Goldlux, weil sie so lecker ist)
nimmt er in seine feuchte Hand
und zerdrückt sie zu Saft.

Er ist neunundzwanzig,
hat Sinn für das Höhere,
schläft schlecht und allein
mit Broschüren und Mitessern,
haßt den Chef und den Supermarkt,
die Kommunisten, die Weiber,
die Hausbesitzer, sich selbst
und seine zerbissenen Fingernägel
voll Margarine (*weil sie
so lecker ist*), brabbelt
unter der Künstlerfrisur
vor sich hin wie ein Greis.

Der
wird es nie zu was bringen.
Schnittler, glaube ich, heißt er,
Schnittler, Hittler, oder so ähnlich.

Portrait of a House Detective

He lolls in the supermarket
under the plastic sun,
the white patches on his face
are rage, not consumption,
a hundred packets of crispy crackers
(*because they're so nourishing*)
he sets ablaze with his eyes,
a piece of margarine
(the same brand as mine:
goldlux, because it's so delicious)
he picks up with his moist hand
and squeezes it till it drips.

He's twenty-nine,
idealistic,
sleeps badly and alone
with brochures and blackheads,
hates the boss and the supermarket,
communists, women,
landlords, himself
and his bitten fingernails
full of margarine (*because
it's so delicious*), under
his arty hairstyle mutters
to himself like a pensioner.

That one
will never get anywhere.
Wittler, I think, he's called,
Wittler, Hittler, or something like that.

Purgatorio

Wehe die Erde ist winzig auf den broschüren
Zur Snackbar watscheln Entwicklungshelfer
eingewickelt in Reiseschecks
Die Quarantäneflagge ist aufgezogen

Herr Albert Schweitzer
wird zur Transit-Auskunft gebeten

Ausgebuchte Buchhalter rudern
durch gläserne Korridore
zum Jüngsten Gericht
Letzter Abruf nach Nagasaki

Herr Adolf Eichmann
wird zur Transit-Auskunft gebeten

Die Welt ist wegen Nebels geschlossen
auf Tretrollern fahren Bräute vor
in wehenden Totenhemden
Die Maschine ist startbereit

Monsieur Godot
wird zur Transit-Auskunft gebeten

Ausgang B Position zweiunddreißig
Die Nylonstimme ruft Weh über uns
Leichenzüge fluten über die Pisten
In der Dunkelheit flammen Sirenen

Purgatorio

Woe the earth is tiny in the brochures
To the snackbar waddle development experts
enveloped in travel cheques
The quarantine flag has been hoisted

Will Herr Albert Schweitzer
please go to Transit Information

Booked out book-keepers paddle
through glass-lined corridors
to the last judgement
Last call for Nagasaki

Will Herr Adolf Eichmann
please go to Transit Information

On account of fog the world is closed
On pedal trolleys brides arrive
in shrouds that trail in the wind
The plane is ready to take off

Will Monsieur Godot
please go to Transit Information

Exit B Channel thirty-two
The nylon voice cries woe upon us
Funeral processions flood the runways
Sirens blaze in the dark

Historischer Prozeß

Die Bucht ist zugefroren.
Die Fischkutter liegen fest.
Das besagt nichts.
Du bist frei.
Du kannst dich hinstrecken.
Du kannst wieder aufstehen.
Es ist nicht schade um deinen Namen.
Du kannst verschwinden
und wiederkommen.
Das ist möglich.
Auch wenn einer stirbt
kommen noch Briefe für ihn.
Es ist nicht viel zu vereiteln.
Du kannst schlafen.
Das ist möglich.
Über Nacht wird der Eisbrecher da sein.
Dann laufen die Kutter aus.
Die Fahrtrinne ist schmal.
Über Nacht friert sie wieder zu.
Das besagt nichts.
Es ist nicht schade um deinen Namen.

Historical Process

The bay is frozen up.
The trawlers are ice-bound.
So what.
You are free.
You can lie down.
You can get up again.
It doesn't matter about your name.
You can disappear
and return.   *not in German*
That's possible.
A fighter howls across the island.
Even when a man dies
letters still come for him.
There isn't much to be lost or thwarted.
You can sleep.
That's possible.
The ice-breaker will be here by the morning.
Then the trawlers will leave.
The channel they follow is narrow.
It freezes up again by the morning.
So what.
It doesn't matter about your name.

Karl Heinrich Marx

Riesiger Großvater
Jahvebärtig
auf braunen Daguerreotypien
Ich seh dein Gesicht
in der schlohweißen Aura
selbstherrlich   streitbar
und die Papiere im Vertiko:
Metzgersrechnungen
Inauguraladressen
Steckbriefe

Deinen massigen Leib
Seh ich im Fahndungsbuch
riesiger Hochverräter
displaced person
in Bratenrock und Plastron
schwindsüchtig   schlaflos
die Galle verbrannt
von schweren Zigarren
Salzgurken   Laudanum
und Likör

Ich seh dein Haus
in der rue d'Alliance
Dean Street   Grafton Terrace
riesiger Bourgeois
Haustyrann
in zerschlissnen Pantoffeln:
Ruß und »ökonomische Scheiße«
Pfandleihen »wie gewöhnlich«
Kindersärge
Hintertreppengeschichten

Keine Mitrailleuse
in deiner Prophetenhand:
ich seh sie ruhig
im British Museum
unter der grünen Lampe

Karl Heinrich Marx

Gigantic grandfather
Jehovah-bearded
on brown daguerrotypes
I see your face
in the snow-white aura
despotic quarrelsome
and your papers in the linen press:
butcher's bills
inaugural addresses
warrants for your arrest

Your massive body
I see in the 'wanted' book
gigantic traitor
displaced person
in tailcoat and plastron
consumptive   sleepless
your gall-bladder scorched
by heavy cigars
salted gherkins   laudanum
and liqueur

I see your house
in the rue d'Alliance
Dean Street   Grafton Terrace
gigantic bourgeois
domestic tyrant
in worn-out slippers:
soot and 'economic shit'
pawnshops 'as usual'
children's coffins
backstair calamities

No machine-gun
in your prophet's hand:
I see it peaceably
in the British Musuem
under the green lamp

mit fürchterlicher Geduld
dein eigenes Haus zerbrechen
riesiger Gründer
andern Häusern zuliebe
in denen du nimmer erwacht bist

Riesiger Zaddik
Ich seh dich verraten
von deinen Anhängern:
nur deine Feinde
sind dir geblieben:
ich seh dein Gesicht
auf dem letzten Bild
vom April zweiundachtzig:
eine eiserne Maske:
die eiserne Maske der Freiheit

break up your own house
with a terrible patience
gigantic founder
for the sake of other houses
in which you never woke up

Gigantic zaddik
I see you betrayed
by your disciples:
only your enemies
remained what they were:
I see your face
on the last picture
of April eighty-two:
an iron mask:
the iron mask of freedom

Lachesis lapponica

Hier ist es hell, am rostigen Wasser, nirgendwo. Hier,
das sind die Grauweiden, das ist das graue Gras,
das ist der düstere helle Himmel, hier stehe ich.

(*Das ist kein Standpunkt*, sagt der Vogel in meinem Kopf.)

Hier wo ich stehe, das Weiße im Wind sind die Moordaunen,
sieh wie es flimmert. Die leere lautlose Wildnis hier ist die Erde.

(*¡Viva!* ruft der düstere Vogel: *¡Viva Fidel Castro!*)

Was hat Castro damit zu schaffen! (*was hast du damit zu schaffen,
mit dem Wollgras, dem Pfeifengras am düsteren Wasser?*)

Nichts, ich habe nichts, Vogel, hörst du? und kein Vogel,
Vogel, kräht nach mir. (*Das ist wahr.*) Laß mich in Ruhe.
Hier kämpfe ich nicht. (Es wird ein Brachvogel sein.)

Dort ist Norden, dort wo es dunkel wird, siehst du,
das Moor wird sehr langsam dunkel. Hier habe ich nichts,
hier habe ich nichts zu tun. Das Weiße im Norden
sind seine Geister, die hellen Geister des Moores.

(*Das ist kein Standpunkt, das sind keine Geister,
das sind Birken*, schreit er, *hier ist nichts los.*)

Das ist gut. Ich kämpfe nicht. Laß mich. Ich warte.

Mit der Zeit, sehr langsam, schält sich die Rinde,
(*ich mache mir nichts daraus*) und das Weiße dort,
das Weiße dort unter dem Weißen, siehst du,
das will ich lesen. (*Und hier*, sagt er, *die genaue Zeit:
dreiundzwanzig Uhr fünfzig.*) Hier, im rostigen Moos.

Ich glaube an Geister (*das gibts nicht!*) leer wild lautlos.
Auch ich bin ein Geist. Auch dieser schreiende Vogel da
in meinem lautlosen Kopf. (*Sag das nicht.*)

Lachesis lapponica

Here it is bright, by the rusty water, nowhere. Here,
these are the grey willows, this is the grey grass,
this is the dusky bright sky, here I stand.

(*That is no standpoint*, says the bird in my head.)

Here where I stand, that whiteness in the wind is the moor sedge,
look how it flickers. The silent empty wilderness here is the earth.

(¡*Viva!* cries the dusky bird: ¡*Viva Fidel Castro!*)

What's Castro got to do with it (*what have you got to do with it,
with the cotton grass, the hair grass by the dusky water?*)

Nothing, I've nothing, bird, do you hear? and no bird,
bird, whistles for me. (*That is true.*) Leave me in peace.
Here I'm not fighting. (It's a curlew, most likely.)

Over there is north, where it's getting dark, you see,
the moor gets dark very slowly. Here I have nothing,
here I have nothing to do. The whiteness up in the north
is the spirits of the north, the moor's bright spirits.

(*That is no standpoint, those are no spirits,
those are birch trees*, it shrieks, *here nothing happens.*)

That's good. I'm not fighting. Leave me. I'm waiting.

In time, very slowly, the bark peels off,
(*it's nothing to me*) and the whiteness there,
the whiteness there under the whiteness, you see,
that I shall read. (*And here*, it says, *the exact time:
twenty-three fifty.*) Here, in the rusty moss.

I believe in spirits (*there's no such thing!*) empty silent wild.
I too am a spirit. And so is that shrieking bird
in my silent head. (*Don't say that.*)

Wir blicken beide nach Norden. Mitternacht. (*am Times Square*
stehst du, Toter, ich kenne dich, sehe dich wie du kaufst,
verkaufst und verkauft wirst, du bist es, auf dem Roten Platz,
auf dem Kurfürstendamm, und blickst auf deine rostige Uhr.)

(ein Brachvogel wird es sein, oder ein Regenpfeifer.
Sag das nicht, schlag dir das aus dem Kopf.)

Ich schlag dir den Kopf ab, Vogel. (*Es ist dein eigner.*
(¡*Viva Fidel! lieber tot als rot! mach mal Pause! Ban the bomb!*
Über alles in der Welt!) Sag das nicht. (*Das alles bist du,*
sagt der Vogel, *stell dir das vor, du bist es gewesen, du bist es.*)

Wie meinst du das? (*Allen Ernstes*, sagt der Vogel und lacht.)
Ein Brachvogel kann nicht lachen. (*Du bist es*, sagt er,
der lacht. Du wirst es bereuen. Ich weiß, wer du bist,
Totenkopf auf dem Kurfürstendamm.) Im Moor.

Weiß, düster, grau. Hier sind keine Siege.
Das sind die Moordaunen, das sind die Grauweiden,
das ist der helle Vogel am düsteren Himmel.

Jetzt ist es Mitternacht, jetzt springt die Rinde,
(*die genaue Zeit:*) es ist weiß, (*null Uhr zwei*)
dort im Rauch, wo es dunkel wird, ist es zu lesen,
das unbeschriebene Blatt. Die leere lautlose Wildnis.
Hier ist nichts los. (*Sag das nicht.*) Hier bin ich.
Laß mich. (*Sag das nicht.*) Laß mich allein.

(*Bist du einverstanden, Totenkopf, bist du tot?*
Ist es ein Regenpfeifer? *Wenn du nicht tot bist,*
worauf wartest du noch?) Ich warte. Ich warte.

Es ist am äußersten Rand dieser Fläche, Sumpfgras,
Wollgras, Pfeifengras, wo es schon düster ist, Vogel,
(*Wie meinst du das?*) Siehst du? Siehst du die weiße Schrift?

(Feigling, sagt er, *machs gut. Wir sprechen uns noch.*)
Laß mich im Unbeschriebenen. (*Totenkopf.*)
Sieh wie es flimmert. (Und der düstere Vogel
in meinem Kopf sagt zu sich selber: *Er schläft, also*
ist er einverstanden.)
            Aber ich schlafe nicht.

We both look northward. Midnight. (*On Times Square*
you stand, dead man, I know you, I see you buy,
sell and be sold, it is you, on Red Square,
on the Kurfürstendamm, and you look at your rusty watch.)

(It's a curlew, most likely, or else a peewit.
Don't say that, get it out of your head.)

I'll cut off your head, bird. (*It's your own.*
¡Viva Fidel! Better dead than red. Have a break! Ban the bomb!
Über alles in der welt!) Don't say that. (*You are all that,*
says the bird, *imagine, you have been that, you are that.*)

How do you mean? (*In all seriousness*, says the bird and laughs.)
A curlew can't laugh. (*It's yourself*, it says,
who are laughing. You'll regret it. I know who you are,
death's head on the Kurfürstendamm.) On the moor.

White, dusky, grey. There are no victories here.
That is the moor sedge, those are the grey willows,
that is the bright bird against the dusky sky.

Now it is midnight, now the bark splits,
(*the exact time:*) it is white, (*zero two minutes*)
there in the mist, where it's getting dark, you can read it,
the blank page. The silent empty wilderness.
Here nothing happens. (*Don't say that.*) Here I am.
Leave me. (*Don't say that.*) Leave me alone.

(*Do you agree with me, death's head, and are you dead?*
Is it a peewit? *If you are not dead*
what are you waiting for?) I'm waiting. I'm waiting.

It is on the outermost edge of this plain, marsh grass,
cotton grass, hair grass, where it is dusky already, bird,
(*How do you mean?*) Do you see? Do you see the white script?

(*Coward*, it says, *good luck. We shall meet again.*)
Leave me where all is blank. (*Death's head.*)
Look how it flickers. (And the dusky bird
in my head says to itself: *He's asleep, that means*
he agrees.)
       But I am not asleep.

Schattenreich

I

Hier sehe ich noch einen Platz,
einen freien Platz,
hier im Schatten.

II

Dieser Schatten
ist nicht zu verkaufen.

III

Auch das Meer
wirft vielleicht einen Schatten,
auch die Zeit.

IV

Die Kriege der Schatten
sind Spiele:
kein Schatten
steht dem andern im Licht.

V

Wer im Schatten wohnt,
ist schwer zu töten.

VI

Für eine Weile
trete ich aus meinem Schatten,
für eine Weile.

VII

Wer das Licht sehen will
wie es ist
muß zurückweichen
in den Schatten.

Shadow Realm

I

Here even now I see a place,
a free place,
here in the shadow.

II

This shadow
is not for sale.

III

The sea too
casts a shadow perhaps,
and so does time.

IV

The wars of shadows
are games:
no shadow
stands in another's light.

V

Those who live in the shadow
are difficult to kill.

VI

For a while
I step out of my shadow,
for a while.

VII

Those who want to see light
as it is
must retire
into the shadow.

VIII

Schatten
heller als diese Sonne:
kühler Schatten der Freiheit.

IX

Ganz im Schatten
verschwindet mein Schatten.

X

Im Schatten
ist immer noch Platz.

VIII

Shadow
brighter than the sun:
cool shadow of freedom.

IX

Completely in the shadow
my shadow disappears.

X

In the shadow
even now there is room.

Die Verschwundenen

für Nelly Sachs

Nicht die Erde hat sie verschluckt. War es die Luft?
Wie der Sand sind sie zahlreich, doch nicht zu Sand
sind sie geworden, sondern zu nichte. In Scharen
sind sie vergessen. Häufig und Hand in Hand,

wie die Minuten. Mehr als wir,
doch ohne Andenken. Nicht verzeichnet,
nicht abzulesen im Staub, sondern verschwunden
sind ihre Namen, Löffel und Sohlen.

Sie reuen uns nicht. Es kann sich niemand
auf sie besinnen: Sind sie geboren,
geflohen, gestorben? Vermißt
sind sie nicht worden. Lückenlos
ist die Welt, doch zusammengehalten
von dem was sie nicht behaust,
von den Verschwundenen. Sie sind überall.

Ohne die Abwesenden wäre nichts da.
Ohne die Flüchtigen wäre nichts fest.
Ohne die Vergessenen nichts gewiß.

Die Verschwundenen sind gerecht.
So verschallen wir auch.

The Vanished

for Nelly Sachs

It wasn't the earth that swallowed them. Was it the air?
Numerous as the sand, they did not become
sand, but came to naught instead. They've been forgotten
in droves. Often, and hand in hand,

like minutes. More than us,
but without memorials. Not registered,
not cipherable from dust, but vanished—
their names, spoons, and footsoles.

They don't make us sorry. Nobody
can remember them: Were they born,
did they flee, have they died? They were
not missed. The world is airtight
yet held together
by what it does not house,
by the vanished. They are everywhere.

Without the absent ones, there would be nothing.
Without the fugitives, nothing is firm.
Without the forgotten, nothing for certain.

The vanished are just.
That's how we'll fade, too.

POEMS 1955–1970

GEDICHTE 1955–1970

(1971)

Sommergedicht

I

Möglich ist alles
          daß wir noch nicht tot sind
Eine Tür öffnet sich
          ein neuer Irrtum
ist mir lieber
          als alle Gewißheiten
in meinem Mund
          ein Geschmack nach früher
Kannst du mir helfen?
          ruft meine Frau
I just hate to be a thing   [Marilyn Monroe
          aus dem Badezimmer
ein Geruch nach Birken
          der Wasserhahn rinnt
Spätnachrichten
          und Vorträge
über Neokapitalismus und Avantgarde

Das ist keine Kunst
          was noch nicht da ist   [Lao Tse
darauf muß man wirken
          ein neuer Irrtum
bricht auf
          die Straßen sind leer
ein Mädchen
          in der kürzesten Nacht des Jahres
fais-moi ça
          fais-moi ça
          auf der Moldau
spielen die Kähne
          die Lichter sind ausgegangen
in einer alten Gasse
          die da heißt
          Die Neue Welt
brechen
          alle Arten von Leidenschaften   [Wieland

Summer Poem

Anything is possible
                that we are not dead yet
A door opens
           and I prefer
new errors
           to every certainty
in my mouth
           a taste of earlier times
Can you help me?
             my wife calls out
I just hate to be a thing   [Marilyn Monroe
           from the bathroom
a smell of birch trees
           the tap is running
late news
      and radio talks
on neo–capitalism and the avant–garde

No great art in that
      one should work upon that   [Lao–Tse
which does not yet exist
           a new error
opens up
        the streets are empty
a girl
      in the shortest night of the year
fais-moi ça
        fais-moi ça
           on the Moldau
the dinghies play
        the lights
            have gone out
in an old street
        which there they call:
                the New World
open

                                        auf
Kannst du mir helfen?
                          in der weißen Nacht
in der Sauna
                    in der Dunkelheit
                                        aah!
eine nie zuvor gekannte Empfindung   [Wieland

Das Große entsteht aus dem Geringen   [Lao Tse
und dazwischen
                          öffnet sich vielleicht
                                        ein Gedicht

     II
Etwas Neues
          ein winziger Schrei
                              bricht auf
etwas Neues
                das alle Springfedern   [Wieland
der Einbildungskraft und des Herzens
zugleich
          in einer alten Gasse
                              spielen macht
im Sonnengeflecht
                    nach der Liebe
ein winziges Gefühl
                    von Unsterblichkeit
das sterblichste aller Gefühle
daß wir noch leben
                    unter soviel toten Leuten
Etwas das früher war
                    wird kleiner
                              und kleiner
und ist verschwunden
                    ein so einziges Schauspiel   [Wieland
wohin
     überall ist es
                    überallhin
                              verschwunden

Ein Geschmack
          am andern Morgen

58

all the varieties of passion   [Wieland

Can you help me?

                in the white night

in the sauna

           in the darkness

                  aah!

a sensation never yet known   [Wieland

From little things grows what is great   [Lao Tse

and in between perhaps

                opens

                    a poem

II

Something new opens

                a tiny cry

something new

                since it brings into play   [Wieland

all the springs of imagination

and of the heart

            in an old street

                    simultaneously

in the solar plexus

            after love

a tiny sensation

            of immortality

the most mortal of all sensations

that we are still alive

                amid so many dead people

Something from earlier times

                grows smaller

                    and smaller

and has disappeared

                a performance so unique   [Wieland

where to

          everywhere it has

                disappeared

                    to everywhere

Next morning

          a taste

nach frischen Erdbeeren
                           die neuen Schlagzeilen
die alte Frage:
                   Kannst du mir helfen?
Ich bin kein Kulturinstitut
                        ich leiste
keine Entwicklungshilfe
                      Erdbeeren
und Apartheid
            Was tun?   [Lenin
                 Eine Ameise
auf der Türschwelle
                  schleppt eine tote Fliege fort
und *Womit beginnen?*   [Lenin
                 Peking
                      Johannesburg
                             überallhin
ist es gleich weit
                    und möglich ist alles
Freedom Now
                 Johannisfeuer
                     Marketing
das ist keine Kunst
                   il parlar rotto   [Petrarca
die Tonbänder zwitschern
                      dazwischen steigt
in seiner ersten Neuheit   [Wieland
                  ein Rezitativ
von Monteverdi auf
                    und beweist nichts
Möglich ist es
                  daß wir noch leben

III

Was noch nicht da ist   [Lao Tse
                    das ist keine Kunst
meine Welt ist so groß
                    in dieser Nacht
wie meine Irrtümer
                  kannst du mir helfen?

Ochsenblutrot

of fresh strawberries
                the new headlines
the old question:
              Can you help me?
I am no cultural institute
                  I offer
no aid for development
                strawberries
and apartheid
           What's to be done?   [Lenin
                      An ant
on the threshold
              drags away a dead fly
and *where to begin?*   [Lenin
              Peking
                    Johannesburg
the distance to every place is the same
                            and anything is
                                possible
Freedom Now
              St John's fire
                  marketing
no great art in that
              il parlar rotto   [Petrarch
the tapes twitter
              in between rises
in its pristine novelty   [Wieland
                a recitativo
by Monteverdi
                    and proves nothing
It is possible
             that we are still alive

    III

That which does not yet exist   [Lao Tse
                    no great art in that
my world is as large
              in this night
as my errors
             can you help me?

Ox-blood red

und verschwunden
das hölzerne Haus
                    ein Bauernmädchen
aus Karelien
                    jetzt ist sie Ansagerin
Spätausgabe
                    Tagesschau
                              in der hellsten Nacht
Fernschreiben auf dem Tisch
                    der Mensch   [Norbert Wiener
eine Nachricht
                    und überallhin
                              ist es gleich weit

Der chinesische Standpunkt
                              und ein winziger Schrei
öffnet sich
          die *New York Times*
                              das *Pekinger Volksblatt*
in meinen Armen
                    dieser Geschmack
                              nach früher
und Birkenlaub
                    in der Sauna
                              die Spätnachrichten
aus dem Geringen das Große   [Lao Tse
Mitternacht
                    hell genug
                              um Zeitung zu lesen
wir sind die Gegenstände
                              der Gegenstände
unseres Denkens
                    Das Elend der Philosophie   [Marx
und *Womit beginnen?*   [Lenin
                    ich habe das alles gelesen
die Straßen sind leer
                    fais-moi ça
das Mögliche
                    öffnet sich
                              die Gräber
unter dem Birkenlaub
                              der frische Mund
der Irrtum
                    die helle Nacht

62

          and disappeared
the wooden house
                    a peasant child
from Karelia
                now she's a news reader
late night
            news bulletin
                        in the brightest night
teleprinter on the table
                    man   [Norbert Wiener
is a message
                and the distance to every place
                                        is the same

The Chinese point of view
                        and a tiny cry
opens
        the *New York Times*
                            the *Peking People's Journal*
in my arms
            this taste
                        of earlier times
and birch leaves
                in the sauna
                            late news
from little things what is great   [Lao Tse
midnight
        bright enough
                        to read a newspaper
we are the subjects
                    of the subjects of our thinking
                the wretchedness of philosophy   [Marx
and *where to begin?*   [Lenin
                I have read it all
the streets are empty
                    fais-moi ça
the possible opens
                    the graves
                            under the birch leaves
the fresh lips
            the error
                        the bright night

                                                            63

IV

(*Wasserhahn Feuerwerk*
                             Ist das dein Ernst?
Birkenlaub ist passé
                      und *Geschmack nach früher:*
das ist keine Kunst
                      sagte der Kritiker
das geht nicht mehr
                      wirf die Metaphern weg
das ist vorbei

Und ich warf die Metaphern weg
                         ging in die Sauna
und fand
           Birkenlaub
                      und diesen Geschmack
nach früher
             in meinem Mund)

V

Schlafen wir also
                    leicht und irrtümlich
und es wecke uns keiner
                        und sage:
Kannst du mir helfen?
                    Hier in diesem Hotel
wird heute nacht
                    niemand erschossen
der Wasserhahn rinnt
                    woanders
der Start
           in die leere Zukunft
Glorien
           Brander
                  und Satelliten
                         aah!
ein so wunderbares Schauspiel   [Wieland

Auch ich bin gefahren
                    in *das*   [Lao Tse
was noch nicht da ist

IV

(*Water tap fireworks*

You can't mean that?

Birch leaves are passé

and *a taste of earlier times:*

no great art in that

said the critic

you can't get away with

that now

throw away the metaphors

they're a thing of the past

And I threw away the metaphors
and went to the sauna

and found

birch leaves

and this taste of earlier times

in my mouth)

V

Let us sleep then

lightly erroneously

and let no one awaken us

saying:

Can you help me?

Here in this hotel

tonight

no one is being shot

the tap is running

elsewhere

the take-off

into an empty future

squibs

golden rain

and satellites

aah!

a performance so wonderful   [Wieland

I too have travelled

to *that*   [Lao Tse

which does not yet exist

durchs Pentagon
auf einem Tretroller
in Tränen
eine nie zuvor gekannte Empfindung [Wieland

Der Touristenkurs hier
ist günstig
für den Irrtum
woanders
finden die Kriege statt
aber überallhin
ist es gleich weit
für den geringen Schrei
die Spätnachrichten
Feuerräder
Schwärmer
und Sonnen
und das Mögliche
hat einen leichten Schlaf
neben mir
In den alten Augen
eines alten Freundes
aus Tilsit
die nicht viel von der Zukunft halten
lese ich
das Geringe [Lao Tse
aus dem das Große entsteht
vielleicht
in der Mitternacht
sitzen wir
Johannes Bobrowski und ich
betrunken
der Wasserhahn rinnt
il subito silenzio [Petrarca
in der Sauna
Kannst du mir helfen?

VI

Ich habe soviel
tote Leute
gesehen
und doch ist noch nichts entschieden

                    through the pentagon
on a treadle scooter
                    in tears
a sensation never yet known   [Wieland

Here the tourist rate of exchange
                              is favourable
to error
          elsewhere
                         the wars take place
but the distance
                         to every place is the same
for the little cry
                    the late news
tourbillions
              nebulae
                         and rockets
and the possible
                    sleeps lightly
                                   at my side
In the ancient eyes
                         of an old friend
from Tilsit
that don't think much of the future
                                   I read
the little things   [Lao Tse
                from which grows what is great
maybe
          at midnight
                         we sit
Johannes Bobrowski and I
                                   drunk
the tap is running
                    il subito silenzio   [Petrarch
in the sauna
              Can you help me?

   VI

I have seen
          so many
                    dead people
and yet nothing has been decided

in diesem Sommer
         mitten im Ausverkauf
Erdbeeren
      Umsätze
         und dieser Geschmack
nach Verschwundenheit
         ist überall
und nach Birkenlaub
Gewisse Sicherheitsfunktionen   [Deutsche Bank AG
        beim Start
ein kleiner Schrei
      gewichtlos
         überall
ist der Mittelpunkt
        und ein neuer Irrtum
steigt feurig auf
      das Mögliche ist
eine Exponentialfunktion
        aller Arten von Leidenschaften   [Wieland
die das Gefühl des Erhabenen
        bei der maschinellen   [Deutsche Bank AG
Bearbeitung der Umsätze
        in der Seele   [Wieland
entzünden kann
      und öffnet sich
          über den Wolken
            aah!
schwebt
    und verschwindet
        hoch
in seiner ersten Neuheit   [Wieland
        über den leeren Straßen
ein Fenster
    öffnet sich
        jemand weint
Über die Behandlung der Widersprüche im Volk   [Mao Tse-Tung

Das Mögliche
      genügt nicht
         Was noch nicht da ist   [Lao Tse
beweist nichts
      die Lichter

this summer
               at the height of the sales
strawberries
               turnovers
                              and this taste
of something disappeared
                              is everywhere
and of birch leaves
certain safety measures   [Deutsche Bank AG
                       at the take-off
a little cry
               weightless
                              everywhere
is the centre
               and a new error
rises fiery
               arc of the possible
exponential function
                              of all the varieties of passion   [Wieland
which can kindle
                       in the mechanical   [Deutsche Bank AG
calculation of turnovers
                              a sense of the sublime   [Wieland
in the soul
               and opens
                              above the clouds
                                             aah!
hovers
       and disappears
                       high up
in its pristine novelty
                              above the empty streets   [Wieland
a window
               opens
                       somebody weeps
about the correct handling of contradictions among the people
                                                    [Mao Tse Tung
The possible
               is not enough
                              That which does not yet exist   [Lao Tse
proves nothing
                       the lights

69

       über der Moldau

i lunghi pianti   [Petrarca
      die Lichter
            sind ausgegangen

VII

Womit beginnen   [Lenin
     in dieser flüchtigen Nacht
am Päijänne-See
      an der Moldau
            oder woanders
mein erbitterter Freund
       betrachtet die Socken
der vorübergehenden
         der *verratenen*   [Trockij
Revolution
     wer stopft sie
        die *Dialektik des Konkreten*   [Karel Kosik
wer flickt sie
      vorübergehende Fehler
und *gewisse Sicherheitsfunktionen*   [Deutsche Bank AG
        bei der maschinellen
Bearbeitung
      der Widersprüche im Volk   [Mao Tse-Tung

Ein neuer Irrtum
      das ist keine Kunst
ein Feuerwerk
     bricht auf
        über dem Fluß
Spiralen
   Glorien
     Sonden
e'l brevissimo riso   [Petrarca
     leuchtet
       steigt
aah!
    Gulasch umd Kommunismus   [Chruscev
        und meine Frau
der Standpunkt der Dritten Welt
        Kannst du
mir helfen?
    Ein Gedicht ist kein Brot

                              over the Moldau
i lunghi pianti   [Petrarch
              the lights
                    have gone out
   VII

Where to begin   [Lenin
              in this brief night
by the Päijänne lake
                    by the Moldau
                              or elsewhere
my embittered friend
                    looks at the socks
of those who passed by
                    of the betrayed   [Trotski
revolution
              who will mend them
              the *dialectic of the concrete*   [Karel Kosik
who will patch them
                    passing errors
and *certain safety measures*   [Deutsche Bank AG
                         in the mechanical
calculation
              of *contradictions among the people*   [Mao Tse Tung

A new error
              no great art in that
a firework
              opens
                    above the river
girandoles
              squibs
                    tourbillons
e'l brevissimo riso   [Petrarch
                    shines
                         rises
aah!
       goulash and communism   [Khrushchev
                         and my wife
the point of view of the third world
                         Can you
help me?
              a poem is not bread

und meine Frau
                 geht langsam
                              über die Brücke
und singt vor sich hin
                           etwas Geringes
das fliegen kann
                 und verschwindet
                           in dem
was noch nicht da ist
                so hell ist die Nacht

VIII

Ein Schritt vorwärts   [Lenin
                zwei Schritte zurück
im schattenbefleckten Laub
                        vor der Orangerie
dein Gesicht in Tränen
                        e i lunghi pianti   [Petrarca
I just hate to be a thing   [Marilyn Monroe

Tarifverhandlungen
                Weizenpreise
                            Dantestudien
ich habe das alles gelesen
                        das ist keine Kunst

Überallhin
                fallen die alten Schatten
an den Rändern
                     brechen neue Irrtümer auf
rascheln
            in unsern Mündern
                       wie Birkenlaub
dieser Geschmack
                in der Nacht
ein Fenster öffnet sich
                ein Gedicht
Über den Widerspruch   [Mao Tse-Tung
                und der jähe Start
                        aah!
ein so großes   [Wieland

and my wife
        walks slowly
                over the bridge
and sings to herself
            something small
that can fly
        and disappears
                in that
which does not yet exist
            so bright the night is

VIII

A step forward   [Lenin
        two steps back
in shade-mottled leafage
                in front of the orangerie
your face bathed in tears
            e i lunghi pianti   [Petrarch
I just hate to be a thing   [Marilyn Monroe

Tariff negotiations
            wheat prices
                  Dante studies
I have read it all
        no great art in that

Everywhere
        the old shadows fall
at the edges
        new errors open
rustle
    in our mouths
            like birch leaves
this taste
        in the night
a window opens
        a poem
about contradiction   [Mao Tse-Tung
        and the sudden take-off
                aah!
a performance   [Wieland

so wunderbares

        so schauerliches

so einziges Schauspiel

            der Start in *das*   [Lao Tse

was noch nicht da ist

        überall

        gleichzeitig

spielen die Rentner Skat

           in Neukölln

ein Feuerwerk

        auf der Moldau

               auf dem Bildschirm

auf dem Päijänne-See

           die Kähne

               spielen

alle Springfedern der Einbildungskraft   [Wieland

beim Start

        in das Reich der Freiheit

vor der Sauna

           Johannisfeuer

              und frische Erdbeeren

auf dem Tisch

        in der kürzesten Nacht

               dieses Jahres (1964)

an den Rändern

        rascheln

             unsere Münder

wie Reispapier

        Nachrichten

             Ratschläge   [Lenin

eines Außenstehenden

        (Finnland 1917)

und ein Irrtum schreit

        fais-moi ça

ein so wunderbares Schauspiel   [Wieland

muß in seiner ersten Neuheit

einen Grad von Entzücken hervorbringen

Ein Gedicht bricht auf

        e'l parlar rotto   [Petrarca

und verschwindet

        e'l subito silenzio

            so wonderful
                        so uncanny
so unique
            the take-off into *that*
which does not yet exist   [Lao Tse
                        everywhere
                        at the same time
the rentiers are playing whist
                        in Neukölln
a firework display
                on the Moldau
                        on the television screen
on the Päijänne lake
                the dinghies
                        play
all the springs of the imagination   [Wieland
at the take-off into
the realm of freedom
                        in front of the sauna
St John's fire
                and fresh strawberries
on the table
                in the shortest night
                        of this year (1964)
at the edges
            rustle
                our mouths
like rice paper
            news
                an outsider's   [Lenin
advice
        (Finland 1917)
and an error screams
                    fais-moi ça
a performance so wonderful   [Wieland
in its pristine novelty must produce
such a degree of rapture

A poem opens
                e'l parlar rotto   [Petrarch
and disappears
                e'l subito silenzio

                                                75

und alles ist möglich
     e'l brevissimo riso
und steigt
    e i lunghi pianti
und verschwindet
      und ist verschwunden

and anything is possible
                    e'l brevissimo riso
and rises
        e i lunghi pianti
and disappears
                and has disappeared

Die Freude

Sie will nicht daß ich von ihr rede
Sie steht nicht auf dem Papier
Sie duldet keinen Propheten

Sie ist eine Fremde
doch ich kenne sie
Ich kenne sie gut

Sie wirft alles um was fest steht
Sie lügt nicht
Sie meutert

Sie allein rechtfertigt mich
Sie ist meine Vernunft
Sie gehört mir nicht

Sie ist fremd und beharrlich
Ich verberge sie
wie eine Schande

Sie ist flüchtig
Niemand kann sie teilen
Niemand kann sie für sich behalten

Ich behalte nichts
Ich teile alles mit ihr
Sie wird fortgehen

Ein anderer wird sie verbergen
auf ihrer siegreichen Flucht
durch die sehr lange Nacht

Joy

She does not want me to speak of her
She won't be put down on paper
She can't stand prophets

She is a stranger
but I know her
I know her well

She will overthrow all that is settled and fast
She will not lie
She will riot

By her alone I am justified
She is my reason, my reason of state
She does not belong to me

She is strange and headstrong
I harbour, I hide her
like a disgrace

She is a fugitive
not to be shared with others
not to be kept for yourself

I keep nothing from her
I share with her all I have
She will leave me

Others will harbour her
on her long flight to victory
and hide her by night

Gedicht über die Zukunft, November 1964

Zwei Männer kommen auf einem Traktor
(Chou En-Lai ist in Moskau)
Zwei Männer in steingrauen Kitteln
(Nobelpreisträger im Frack)
Zwei Männer mit dünnen Stecken
(Goldmedaillen aus Tokio)
am Straßenrand zwischen gelben Blättern
(die toten Guerrilleros von Vietnam)

Zwischen die lehmgelben Blätter
stecken zwei Männer in grauen Kitteln
am Straßenrand dünne Stöcke
alle fünfzig Schritt einen links einen rechts
dunkle Stöcke im hellen November
(Chou En-Lai ist in Moskau)

Zwei Männer in grauen Kitteln
riechen im flachen Novemberlicht
den Schnee der zudecken wird
Blätter und Männer

bis kein Weg mehr zu sehen ist
nur noch alle fünfzig Schritt
ein dünner Stock links
ein dünner Stock rechts
damit der Schneepflug
wo kein Weg mehr zu sehen ist
einen Weg finde

Poem about the Future, November 1964

Two men appear on a tractor
(Chou En-Lai is in Moscow)
Two men in stone-grey overalls
(Nobel Prize winners in evening dress)
Two men with slender sticks
(gold medals from Tokyo)
at the wayside amid yellow leaves
(the dead guerillas of Vietnam)

Among the clay-yellow leaves
two men in grey overalls
put up slender sticks at the wayside
one left one right every fifty paces
dark sticks in bright November
(Chou En-Lai is in Moscow)

Two men in grey overalls
scent in the shallow November light
the snow that will cover
leaves and men

till no way is to be seen
only at every fiftieth pace
a slender stick on the left
a slender stick on the right
so that the snow-plough
will find a way
where no way is to be seen

Lied von denen auf die alles zutrifft
und die alles schon wissen

Daß etwas getan werden muß und zwar sofort
das wissen wir schon
daß es aber noch zu früh ist um etwas zu tun
daß es aber zu spät ist um noch etwas zu tun
das wissen wir schon

und daß es uns gut geht
und daß es so weiter geht
und daß es keinen Zweck hat
das wissen wir schon

und daß wir schuld sind
und daß wir nichts dafür können daß wir schuld sind
und daß wir daran schuld sind daß wir nichts dafür können
und daß es uns reicht
das wissen wir schon

und daß es vielleicht besser wäre die Fresse zu halten
und daß wir die Fresse nicht halten werden
das wissen wir schon
das wissen wir schon

und daß wir niemand helfen können
und daß uns niemand helfen kann
das wissen wir schon

und daß wir begabt sind
und daß wir die Wahl haben zwischen nichts und wieder nichts
und daß wir dieses Problem gründlich analysieren müssen
und daß wir zwei Stück Zucker in den Tee tun
das wissen wir schon

und daß wir gegen die Unterdrückung sind
und daß die Zigaretten teurer werden
das wissen wir schon

Song for Those Who Know

Something must be done right away
that much we know
but of course it's too soon to act
but of course it's too late in the day
oh we know

we know that we're really rather well off
and that we'll go on like this
and that it's not much use anyway
oh we know

we know that we are to blame
and that it's not our fault if we are to blame
and that we're to blame for the fact that it's not our fault
and that we're fed up with it
oh we know

and that maybe it would be a good idea to keep our mouths shut
and that we won't keep our mouths shut all the same
oh we know
oh we know

and we also know that we can't help anybody really
and that nobody really can help us
oh we know

and that we're extremely gifted and brilliant
and free to choose between nothing and naught
and that we must analyse this problem very carefully
and that we take two lumps of sugar in our tea
oh we know

we know all about oppression
and that we are very much against it
and that cigarettes have gone up again
oh we know

und daß wir es jedesmal kommen sehen
und daß wir jedesmal recht behalten werden
und daß daraus nichts folgt
das wissen wir schon

und daß das alles wahr ist
das wissen wir schon

und daß das alles gelogen ist
das wissen wir schon

und daß das alles ist
das wissen wir schon

und daß Überstehn nicht alles ist sondern gar nichts
das wissen wir schon

und daß wir es uberstehn
das wissen wir schon

und daß das alles nicht neu ist
und daß das Leben schön ist
das wissen wir schon
das wissen wir schon
das wissen wir schon

und daß wir das schon wissen
das wissen wir schon

we see it coming evry time

not in German

we know very well that the nation is heading for real trouble
and that our forecasts have usually been dead right *nothing comes from this*
and that they are not of any use
and that all this is just talk —— *not in German*
oh we know

survive

that it's just not good enough to live things down
and that we are going to live them down all the same
oh we know oh we know *survive*

that there is nothing new in all this
and that life is wonderful
and that's all there is to it
oh we know all this perfectly well

and that we know all this perfectly well
oh we know that too
oh we know it
oh we know

Rondeau

Reden ist leicht.

Aber Wörter kann man nicht essen.
Also backe Brot.
Brot backen ist schwer.
Also werde Bäcker.

Aber in einem Brot kann man nicht wohnen.
Also bau Häuser.
Häuser bauen ist schwer.
Also werde Maurer.

Aber auf einen Berg kann man kein Haus bauen.
Also versetze den Berg.
Berge versetzen ist schwer.
Also werde Prophet.

Aber Gedanken kann man nicht hören.
Also rede.
Reden ist schwer.
Also werde was du bist

und murmle weiter vor dich hin,
unnützes Geschöpf.

Rondeau

It's easy to talk.

But you can't eat words.
So bake bread.
It's hard to bake bread.
So become a baker.

But you can't live in a loaf.
So build houses.
It's hard to build houses.
So become a bricklayer.

But you can't build a house on a mountain.
So move the mountain.
It's hard to move mountains.
So become a prophet.

But you can't hear thoughts.
So talk.
It's hard to talk.
So become what you are

and keep on muttering to yourself,
useless creature.

Die Macht der Gewohnheit

Gewohnheit macht den Fehler schön.
CHRISTIAN FÜRCHTEGOTT GELLERT

I

Gewöhnliche Menschen haben für gewöhnlich
für gewöhnliche Menschen nichts übrig.
Und umgekehrt.
Gewöhnliche Menschen finden es ungewöhnlich,
daß man sie ungewöhnlich findet.
Schon sind sie keine gewöhnlichen Menschen mehr.
Und umgekehrt.

II

Daß man sich an alles gewöhnt,
daran gewöhnt man sich.
Man nennt das gewöhnlich
einen Lernprozeß.

III

Es ist schmerzlich,
wenn der gewohnte Schmerz ausbleibt.
Wie müde ist das aufgeweckte Gemüt
seiner Aufgewecktheit!
Der einfache Mensch da z. B. findet es schwierig,
ein einfacher Mensch zu sein,
während jene komplexe Persönlichkeit
ihre Schwierigkeiten herleiert
wie die Betschwester den Rosenkranz.
Überall diese ewigen Anfänger,
die längst am Ende sind.
Auch der Haß ist eine liebe Gewohnheit.

IV

Das noch nie Dagewesene
sind wir gewohnt.
Das noch nie Dagewesene
ist ein Gewohnheitsrecht.

The Force of Habit

Habit makes beautiful the fault.
CHRISTIAN FÜRCHTEGOTT GELLERT

I

Ordinary people ordinarily do not care
for ordinary people.
And vice versa.
Ordinary people find it extraordinary
that people find them extraordinary.
At once they have ceased to be ordinary.
And vice versa.

II

That one gets used to everything—
one gets used to that.
The usual name for it is
a learning process.

III

It is painful
when the habitual pain does not present itself.
How tired the lively mind
is of its liveliness!
The simple person there for instance finds it complicated
to be a simple person,
while that complex character
rattles of his complexity
as nuns do their rosaries.
All these eternal beginners
who long ago reached the end.
Hatred, too, is a precious habit.

IV

The utterly unprecedented—
we are used to that.
The utterly unprecedented
is our habitual right.

Ein Gewohnheitstier
trifft an der gewohnten Ecke
einen Gewohnheitsverbrecher.
Eine unerhörte Begebenheit.
Die gewöhnliche Scheiße.
Die Klassiker waren gewöhnt,
Novellen daraus zu machen.

V

Sanft ruhet die Gewohnheit der Macht
auf der Macht der Gewohnheit.

A creature of habit
at the usual corner meets
an habitual criminal.
An unheard-of occurrence.
The usual shit.
Our 'classics' were in the habit
of turning it into stories.

V

Untroubled the habit of force reposes
on the force of habit.

Hommage à Gödel

Münchhausens Theorem, Pferd, Sumpf und Schopf,
ist bezaubernd, aber vergiß nicht:
Münchhausen war ein Lügner.

Gödels Theorem wirkt auf den ersten Blick
etwas unscheinbar, doch bedenk:
Gödel hat recht.

»In jedem genügend reichhaltigen System
lassen sich Sätze formulieren,
die innerhalb des Systems
weder beweis- noch widerlegbar sind,
es sei denn das System
wäre selber inkonsistent.«

Du kannst deine eigene Sprache
in deiner eigenen Sprache beschreiben:
aber nicht ganz.
Du kannst dein eignes Gehirn
mit deinem eignen Gehirn erforschen:
aber nicht ganz.
Usw.

Um sich zu rechtfertigen
muß jedes denkbare System
sich transzendieren,
d.h. zerstören.

»Genügend reichhaltig« oder nicht:
Widerspruchsfreiheit
ist eine Mangelerscheinung
oder ein Widerspruch.

(Gewißheit = Inkonsistenz.)

Jeder denkbare Reiter,
also auch Münchhausen,
also auch du bist ein Subsystem
eines genügend reichhaltigen Sumpfes.

Homage to Gödel

'Pull yourself out of the mire
by your own hair': Münchausen's theorem
is charming, but do not forget:
the Baron was a great liar.

Gödel's theorem may seem, at first sight,
rather nondescript,
but please keep in mind:
Gödel is right.

'In any sufficiently rich system
statements are possible
which can neither be proved
nor refuted within the system,
unless the system itself
is inconsistent.'

You can describe your own language
in your own language:
but not quite.
You can investigate your own brain
by means of your own brain:
but not quite.
Etc.

In order to be vindicated
any conceivable system
must transcend, and that means,
destroy itself.

'Sufficiently rich' or not:
Freedom from contradiction
is either a deficiency symptom,
or it amounts to a contradiction.

(Certainty = Inconsistency.)

Any conceivable horseman,
including Münchausen,
including yourself, is a subsystem
of a sufficiently rich mire.

Und ein Subsystem dieses Subsystems
ist der eigene Schopf,
dieses Hebezeug
für Reformisten und Lügner.

In jedem genügend reichhaltigen System,
also auch in diesem Sumpf hier,
lassen sich Sätze formulieren,
die innerhalb des Systems
weder beweis- noch widerlegbar sind.

Diese Sätze nimm in die Hand
und zieh!

And a subsystem of this subsystem
is your own hair,
favourite tackle
of reformists and liars.

In any sufficiently rich system
including the present mire
statements are possible
which can neither be proved
nor refuted within the system.

Those are the statements
to grasp, and pull!

Wunschkonzert

Samad sagt Gib mir einen Fladen Brot
Frl. Brockmann sucht eine gemütliche kleine Komfortwohnung
    nicht zu teuer mit Kochnische und Besenkammer
Veronique sehnt sich nach der Weltrevolution
Dr Luhmann möchte unbedingt mit seiner Mamma schlafen
Uwe Köpke träumt von einem Kabinettstück Thurn und Taxis
    sieben Silbergroschen hellblau ungezähnt
Simone weiß ganz genau was sie will Berühmt sein Einfach berühmt
    sein ganz egal wofür und um welchen Preis
Wenn es nach Konrad ginge bliebe er einfach im Bett liegen
Mrs Woods möchte andauernd gefesselt und vergewaltigt werden
    aber nur von hinten und nur von einem Gentleman
Guido Ronconis einziger Wunsch ist die unio mystica
Fred Podritzke schlüge am liebsten mit einem Gasrohr auf all diese
    Spinner ein bis sich keiner mehr rührte
Wenn er jetzt nicht sofort sein Sahneschnitzel mit Gurkensalat
    bekommt wird Karel aber durchdrehen
Was Buck braucht ist ein Flash und sonst nichts

Und Friede auf Erden und ein Heringsbrötchen und den herr-
    schaftsfreien Diskurs und ein Baby und eine Million steuer-
    frei und ein Stöhnen das in die bekannten kleinen atemlosen
    Schreie übergeht und einen Pudel aus Plüsch und Freiheit
    für alle und Kopf ab und daß uns die ausgefallenen Haare
    wieder nachwachsen über Nacht

Concert of Wishes

Samad says: Give me my daily pita
Fräulein Brockmann looks for a comfortable little flat not too ex-
    pensive with a cooking recess and a broom cupboard
Véronique longs for world revolution
Dr Luhmann desperately needs to sleep with his mum
Uwe Köpke dreams of a perfect specimen of Thurn and Taxis seven
    silbergroschen pale blue imperforated
Simone knows exactly what she wants: to be famous Simply famous
    no matter what for or at what price
If Konrad had his way he'd simply lie in bed for ever
Mrs Woods would like to be tied up and raped quite regularly but
    only from behind and by a gentleman
Guido Ronconi's only desire is the unio mystica
Fred Podritzke would love to work over all those crackpot lefties with
    a length of gas piping until not one of them so much as twitches
If someone doesn't give him his steak and chips this minute Karel
    will blow his top
What Buck needs is a flash and nothing else

And peace on earth and a ham sandwich and the uncensored dia-
    logue and a baby and a million free of tax and a moaning that
    gives way to the familiar little breathless shrieks and a plush
    poodle and freedom for all and off with his head and that the
    hair we have lost will grow again overnight

THE SINKING OF THE TITANIC

DER UNTERGANG DER TITANIC

(1978)

Apokalypse. Umbrisch, etwa 1490

Er ist nicht mehr der Jüngste, er seufzt,
er holt eine große Leinwand hervor, er grübelt,
verhandelt lang und zäh mit dem Besteller,
einem geizigen Karmeliter aus den Abruzzen,
Prior oder Kapitular. Schon wird es Winter,
die Fingergelenke knacken, das Reisig
knackt im Kamin. Er seufzt, grundiert,
läßt trocknen, grundiert ein andermal,
kritzelt, ungeduldig, auf kleine Kartons
seine Figuren, schemenhaft, hebt sie mit Deckweiß.
Er zaudert, reibt Farben an, vertrödelt
mehrere Wochen. Dann, eines Tages, es ist
unterdessen Aschermittwoch geworden
oder Mariä Lichtmeß, taucht er, in aller Frühe,
den Pinsel in die gebrannte Umbra und malt:
Das wird ein dunkles Bild. Wie fängt man es an,
den Weltuntergang zu malen? Die Feuersbrünste,
die entflohenen Inseln, die Blitze, die sonderbar
allmählich einstürzenden Mauern, Zinnen und Türme:
technische Fragen, Kompositionsprobleme.
Die ganze Welt zu zerstören macht viel Arbeit.
Besonders schwer sind die Geräusche zu malen,
das Zerreißen des Vorhangs im Tempel,
die brüllenden Tiere, der Donner. Alles
soll nämlich zerreißen, zerrissen werden,
nur nicht die Leinwand. Und der Termin
steht fest: Allerspätestens Allerseelen.
Bis dahin muß, im Hintergrund, das wütende Meer
lasiert werden, tausendfach, mit grünen,
schaumigen Lichtern, durchbohrt von Masten,
lotrecht in die Tiefe schießenden Schiffen,
Wracks, während draußen, mitten im Juli,
kein Hund sich regt auf dem staubigen Platz.
Der Maler ist ganz allein in der Stadt geblieben,
verlassen von Frauen, Schülern, Gesinde.
Müde scheint er, wer hätte das gedacht,
sterbensmüde. Alles ist ocker, schattenlos,
steht starr da, hält still in einer Art

Apocalypse. Umbrian Master, about 1490

He is not as young as he used to be. With a groan
he chooses a sizeable canvas. He broods on it.
He wastes his time haggling about his commission
with a mean Carmelite monk from the Abruzzi,
prior, or canon, or whatnot. It is winter now.
His finger joints start cracking like the brushwood
in the fireplace. With a groan he will ground
the canvas, let it dry, ground it once more,
will scrawl his figures, impatiently, ghostlike,
on small cartoons, and set them off with white lead.
He temporises and idles away a few weeks,
rubbing down his colours. But at long last—
Ash Wednesday has gone by, and Candlemas—
early one morning he dips his brush in burnt umber
and starts painting. This will be a gloomy picture.
How do you go about painting Doom? The conflagrations,
the vanishing islands, the lightning, the walls
and towers and pinnacles crumbling ever so slowly:
nice points of technique, problems of composition.
Destroying the world is a difficult exercise.
Hardest to paint are the sounds—for example
the temple veil being rent asunder, the beasts
roaring, and the thunderclaps. Everything, you see,
is to be rent asunder and torn to pieces,
except the canvas. And there can be no doubt
about the appointed time: by All Souls' Day
the frantic sea in the background must be coated
over and over again with a thousand layers
of transparency, with foamy green lights,
pierced by mastheads, by ships reeling, plunging down,
by wrecks, while outside, in mid-July,
not a dog will stir on the dust-covered square.
The women have left, the servants, the disciples.
In the forlorn town only the Master remains.
He looks tired. Who would have thought that he, of all people,
would look dead tired? Ochre—everything seems ochre now,
shadowless, standing still, transfixed in a kind
of evil eternity, except the picture. It grows

böser Ewigkeit; nur das Bild nicht. Das Bild
nimmt zu, verdunkelt sich langsam, füllt sich
mit Schatten, stahlblau, erdgrau, trübviolett,
caput mortuum; füllt sich mit Teufeln, Reitern,
Gemetzeln; bis daß der Weltuntergang
glücklich vollendet ist, und der Maler
erleichtert, für einen kurzen Augenblick;
unsinnig heiter, wie ein Kind,
als wär ihm das Leben geschenkt,
lädt er, noch für denselben Abend,
Frauen, Kinder, Freunde und Feinde
zum Wein, zu frischen Trüffeln und Bekassinen,
während draußen der erste Herbstregen rauscht.

and darkens slowly, absorbing shadows,
steel-blue; livid, dull violet, caput mortuum,
absorbing demons and horsemen and massacres,
until Doom is happily consummated and the artist,
for a brief moment, is, like a child, unmindfully merry,
as if his life had been spared, and in his relief
on this very night he asks his friends to a feast
and treats them to truffles, to grouse and old wine,
with the season's first rainstorm pounding away at the shutters.

Verlustanzeige

Die Haare verlieren, die Nerven,
versteht ihr, die kostbare Zeit,
auf verlorenem Posten an Höhe
verlieren, an Glanz, ich bedaure,
macht nichts, nach Punkten,
unterbrecht mich nicht, Blut
verlieren, Vater und Mutter,
das in Heidelberg verlorene Herz,
ohne mit der Wimper zu zucken,
noch einmal verlieren, den Reiz
der Neuheit, Schwamm drüber,
die bürgerlichen Ehrenrechte, aha,
den Kopf, in Gottesnamen, den Kopf,
wenn es unbedingt sein muß,
das verlorene Paradies, meinetwegen,
den Arbeitsplatz, den Verlorenen Sohn,
das Gesicht, auch das noch,
einen Backenzahn, zwei Weltkriege,
drei Kilo Übergewicht verlieren,
verlieren, immer nur verlieren, auch
die längst verlorenen Illusionen,
na wenn schon, kein Wort
über die verlorene Liebesmüh,
aber woher denn, das Augenlicht
aus den Augen, die Unschuld
verlieren, schade, den Hausschlüssel,
schade, sich, gedankenverloren,
in der Menge verlieren,
unterbrecht mich nicht,
den Verstand, den letzten Heller,
sei's drum, gleich bin ich fertig,
die Fassung, Hopfen und Malz,
alles auf einmal verlieren,
wehe, sogar den Faden,
den Führerschein, und die Lust.

Notice of Loss

To lose your hair, to lose your temper,
if you see what I mean, your precious time,
to fight a losing battle,
losing height and lustre, sorry,
never mind, to lose on points,
let me bloody well finish,
to lose blood, father and mother,
to lose your heart, lost long ago
in Heidelberg, all over again,
without batting an eye, the charm
of novelty, forget it, to lose
civic rights, I get the message,
to lose your head, by all means,
if it can't be helped,
to lose Paradise Lost, what next,
your job, the Prodigal Son,
to lose face, good riddance,
two World Wars, one molar,
seven pounds of overweight,
to lose, lose, and lose again, even
your illusions long ago lost,
so what, let us not waste another word
on love's labour lost, I should say not,
to lose sight of your lost sight,
your virginity, what a pity, your keys,
what a pity, to get lost in the crowd,
lost in thoughts, let me finish,
to lose your mind, your last penny,
no matter, I'll be through in a moment,
your lost causes, all sense of shame,
everything, blow by blow,
alas, even the thread of your story,
your driver's licence, your soul.

Abendmahl. Venezianisch, 16. Jahrhundert

I

Als ich mein *Letztes Abendmahl* beendet hatte,
fünfeinhalb mal knapp dreizehn Meter,
eine Heidenarbeit, aber ganz gut bezahlt,
kamen die üblichen Fragen.
Was haben diese Ausländer zu bedeuten
mit ihren Hellebarden? Wie Ketzer
sind sie gekleidet, oder wie Deutsche.
Finden Sie es wohl schicklich,
dem Heiligen Lukas
einen Zahnstocher in die Hand zu geben?
Wer hat Sie dazu angestiftet,
Mohren, Säufer und Clowns
an den Tisch Unseres Herrn zu laden?
Was soll dieser Zwerg mit dem Papagei,
was soll der schnüffelnde Hund,
und warum blutet der Mameluck aus der Nase?
Meine Herrn, sprach ich, dies alles
habe ich frei erfunden zu meinem Vergnügen.
Aber die Sieben Richter der Heiligen Inquisition
raschelten mit ihren roten Roben
und murmelten: Überzeugt uns nicht.

II

Oh, ich habe bessere Bilder gemalt;
aber jener Himmel zeigt Farben,
die ihr auf keinem Himmel findet,
der nicht von mir gemalt ist;
und es gefallen mir diese Köche
mit ihren riesigen Metzgersmessern,
diese Leute mit Diademen, mit Reiherbüschen,
pelzverbrämten, gezaddelten Hauben
und perlenbestickten Turbanen;
auch jene Vermummten gehören dazu,
die auf die entferntesten Dächer
meiner Alabaster-Päläste geklettert sind
und sich über die höchsten Brüstungen beugen.

Last Supper. Venetian, Sixteenth Century

I

As soon as I had finished my *Last Supper*
thirteen yards by five and a half,
a monstrous job, but rather well paid,
the usual questions came up:
What exactly are these foreigners doing here
with their halberds? They are dressed
like Germans, or like heretics.
Do you think it is normal
to depict Saint Luke
with a toothpick in his hand?
Who put the idea into your head
to sit Moors, drunkards and clowns
at Our Lord's table?
Do we have to put up with a dog
sniffing around, a dwarf, a parrot
and a Mameluke bleeding from his nose?
My Lords, I said, all this
I have invented for my own pleasure.
But the seven judges of the Holy Inquisition,
in a flutter of red silk robes,
murmured: That's as may be.

II

Oh, I have done better than that
in other paintings,
but nobody else can do a sky
the colour of this one;
and I am pleased by these cooks
with their long butcher's knives,
by these men clad in slashed hoods
trimmed with fur, in aigrets
adorned with heron feathers, in diadems
and pearl-studded turbans;
not to mention the muffled people
who have mounted the most distant rooftops
of my alabaster-faced palaces,

Wonach sie Ausschau halten,
das weiß ich nicht. Aber weder euch
noch den Heiligen schenken sie einen Blick.

III

Wie oft soll ich es euch noch sagen!
Es gibt keine Kunst ohne das Vergnügen.
Das gilt auch für die endlosen Kreuzigungen,
Sintfluten und Bethlehemitischen Kindermorde,
die ihr, ich weiß nicht warum,
bei mir bestellt.
Als die Seufzer der Kritiker,
die Spitzfindigkeiten der Inquisitoren
und die Schnüffeleien der Schriftgelehrten
mir endlich zu dumm wurden,
taufte ich das *Letzte Abendmahl* um
und nannte es
Ein Dîner bei Herrn Levi.

IV

Wir werden ja sehen, wer den längeren Atem hat.
Zum Beispiel meine *Heilige Anna selbdritt.*
Kein sehr amüsantes Sujet.
Doch unter den Thron,
auf den herrlich gemusterten Marmorboden
in Sandrosa, Schwarz und Malachit,
malte ich, um das Ganze zu retten,
eine Suppenschildkröte mit rollenden Augen,
zierlichen Füßen und einem Panzer
aus halb durchsichtigem Schildpatt:
eine wunderbare Idee.
Wie ein riesiger, kunstvoll gewölbter Kamm,
topasfarben, glühte sie in der Sonne.

V

Als ich sie kriechen sah,
fielen mir meine Feinde ein.
Ich hörte das Gebrabbel der Galeristen,
das Zischeln der Zeichenlehrer
und das Rülpsen der Besserwisser.

leaning over the parapets at a dizzy height.
What they are looking for
I cannot tell. But they do not even glance
at you, or at the saints.

III

I have told you again and again:
There is no art without pleasure.
This is true even of the endless Crucifixions,
Deluges and Massacres of the Innocent
which you ask me to execute –
I cannot imagine why.
So when the sighs of the critics,
the subtleties of the inquisitors
and the probings of the scribes
became too much for me,
I rechristened my *Last Supper*
and decided to call it
A Dinner at Mr Levi's.

IV

Just wait and see who will have the last word.
Take my *Saint Anne, the Virgin and Child*, for example.
Not a very amusing subject.
But underneath the throne,
on the checkered marble floor
done in sand-rose, black and malachite,
I put, as a redeeming grace,
a soup turtle with rolling eyes,
elegant feet and a shield
of translucent tortoiseshell.
A marvellous idea.
Like an enormous, perfectly arched shell comb,
the colour of topaz, she glowed in the sun.

V

But as soon as I saw her crawling,
I thought of my enemies.
The gallerists babbling,
the academicians hissing,
and the belching of the prigs.

Ich nahm meinen Pinsel zur Hand
und begrub das Geschöpf,
bevor die Schmarotzer anfangen konnten,
mir zu erklären, was es bedeute,
unter sorgfältig gemalten Fliesen
aus schwarzem, grünem und rosa Marmor.
Die *Heilige Anna* ist nicht mein berühmtestes,
aber vielleicht mein bestes Bild.
Keiner außer mir weiß, warum.

I took up my brush
and I buried my creature
beneath a few carefully done tiles
of black, green and rose-coloured marble
before the parasites had a chance
to explain her to me.
Saint Anne is not my most famous work,
but perhaps my best.
No one except me knows why.

Innere Sicherheit

Ich versuche den Deckel zu heben,
logischerweise, den Deckel,
der meine Kiste verschließt.
Es ist ja kein Sarg, das nicht,
es ist nur eine Packung, eine Kabine,
mit einem Wort, eine Kiste.

Ihr wißt doch genau, was ich meine,
wenn ich *Kiste* sage,
stellt euch nicht dumm,
ich meine ja nur
eine ganz gewöhnliche Kiste,
auch nicht dunkler als eure.

Also ich möchte raus, ich klopfe,
ich hämmere gegen den Deckel,
ich rufe *Mehr Licht*, ich ringe
nach Atem, logischerweise,
ich donnere gegen die Luke. Gut.

Aber sicherheitshalber ist sie zu,
meine Kiste, sie geht nicht auf,
mein Schuhkarton hat einen Deckel,
der Deckel aber ist ziemlich schwer,
aus Sicherheitsgründen,
denn es handelt sich hier
um einen Behälter, um eine Bundeslade,
um einen Safe. Ich schaffe es nicht.

Die Befreiung kann, logischerweise,
nur mit vereinter Kraft gelingen.
Aber sicherheitshalber bin ich
in meiner Kiste mit mir allein,
in meiner eigenen Kiste.

Security Considerations

I am trying to lift the lid,
logically, the lid
on my private crate.
It isn't a coffin by any means,
it is just a package, a cabin, or
in a word, a crate.

You know what I mean
when I say *crate*, come on,
don't play the fool,
all I mean
is an average crate,
just as dark as your own.

Of course I want to get out,
and therefore I knock,
I hammer against the lid,
I call out *More light*, I gasp,
logically, pounding away at the hatch.

So far so good. Unfortunately,
for security reasons,
my crate does not open,
my shoe box has a lid,
a rather heavy one to be sure,
for security reasons,
since we are dealing here
with a container, an Ark
of the Covenant, a safe.
There is no way out.

For our liberation, joint action
would, logically, be needed.
But for security reasons
I am all alone in my crate,
in my very own crate.

Jedem das Seine! Um mit vereinter Kraft
zu entweichen aus der eigenen Kiste,
müßte ich, logischerweise, bereits
aus der eigenen Kiste
entwichen sein, und das gilt,
logischerweise, für alle.

Also stemme ich mich gegen den Deckel
mit meinem eignen Genick. Jetzt!
Einen Spalt breit! Ah! Draußen,
herrlich, die weite Landschaft,
bedeckt mit Büchsen, Kanistern,
kurzum, mit Kisten, dahinter
die eifrig rollenden grünen Fluten,
durchpflügt von seetüchtigen Koffern,
die unerhört hohen Wolken darüber,
und überall, überall Luft!

Laßt mich raus, rufe ich also,
erlahmend, wider besseres Wissen,
mit belegter Zunge, von Schweiß bedeckt.
Ein Kreuz schlagen, kommt nicht in Frage.
Winken, geht nicht, keine Hand frei.
Die Faust ballen, ausgeschlossen.

Also, *Ich drücke*, rufe ich,
mein Bedauern aus, wehe mir!
mein eignes Bedauern,
während mit dumpfem *Pflupp*
der Deckel sich wieder,
aus Sicherheitsgründen,
über mir schließt.

To every man his due! And hence,
for me to escape, by joint action,
from my own crate, logically
I would have to be out of it
to start with, and this condition obtains,
logically, for all of us.

Thus I break my very own back
against the lid. Now!
A chink, a narrow gap! Ah!
Marvellous! The open country
outside, covered with tins,
containers, or just plain crates,
in the background the high-rolling waves
ploughed by seaworthy trunks,
the enormously distant clouds above,
and lots and lots of fresh air!

Let me out, I proceed to cry,
feebly, with my tongue coated, against
my better judgement, covered with sweat.
To make the sign of the cross: impossible.
To beckon: no, I am short of hands.
To clench the fist: out of the question.

And hence I cry: *I express
my regrets, woe to me,
my very own regrets*,
while with a hollow *plop*
the lid, for security reasons,
comes down again
over my head.

Der Aufschub

Bei dem berühmten Ausbruch des Helgafell, eines Vulkans
auf der Insel Heimaey, live übertragen von einem Dutzend
hustender Fernsehteams, sah ich, unter dem Schwefelregen,
einen älteren Mann in Hosenträgern, der, achselzuckend
und ohne sich weiter zu kümmern um Sturmwind, Hitze,
Kameraleute, Asche, Zuschauer (unter ihnen auch ich
vor dem bläulichen Bildschirm auf meinem Teppich).
mit einem Gartenschlauch, dünn aber deutlich sichtbar,
gegen die Lava vorging, bis endlich Nachbarn, Soldaten,
Schulkinder, ja sogar Feuerwehrleute mit Schläuchen,
immer mehr Schläuchen, gegen die heiße, unaufhaltsam
vorrückende Lava eine Mauer aus naß erstarrter
kalter Lava höher und höher türmten, und so,
zwar aschgrau und nicht für immer, doch einstweilen,
den Untergang des Abendlandes aufschoben, dergestalt,
daß, falls sie nicht gestorben sind, auf Heimaey,
einer Insel unweit von Island, heute noch diese Leute
in ihren kleinen bunten Holzhäusern morgens erwachen
und nachmittags, unbeachtet von Kameras, den Salat
in ihren Gärten, lavagedüngt und riesenköpfig,
sprengen, vorläufig nur, natürlich, doch ohne Panik.

The Reprieve

Watching the famous eruption of a volcano on Heimaey, Iceland,
which was broadcast live by any number of TV teams,
I saw an elderly man in braces showered by sulphur and brimstone,
ignoring the storm, the heat, the video cables, the ash
and the spectators (including myself, crouching on my carpet
in front of the livid screen), who held a garden hose,
slender but clearly visible, aimed at the roaring lava,
until neighbours joined him, soldiers, children, firemen,
pointing more and more hoses at the advancing fiery lava
and turning it into a towering wall, higher and higher,
of lava, hard, cold and wet, the colour of ash, and thus postponing,
not forever perhaps, but for the time being at least,
the Decline of Western Civilisation, which is why
the people of Heimaey, unless they have died since,
continue to dwell unmolested by cameras
in their dapper white wooden houses,
calmly watering in the afternoon
the lettuce in their gardens, which, thanks to the blackened soil,
has grown simply enormous, and for the time being at least,
fails to show any signs of impending disaster.

Schwacher Trost

Der Kampf aller gegen alle soll,
wie aus Kreisen verlautet,
die dem Innenministerium nahestehn,
demnächst verstaatlicht werden,
bis auf den letzten Blutfleck.
Schöne Grüße von Hobbes.

Bürgerkrieg mit ungleichen Waffen:
was dem einen die Steuererklärung,
ist dem andern die Fahrradkette.
Die Giftmischer und die Brandstifter
werden eine Gewerkschaft gründen müssen
zum Schutz ihrer Arbeitsplätze.

Aufgeschlossen bis dort hinaus
geht es im Strafvollzug zu.
Abwaschbar, in schwarzes Plastik gebunden,
liegt Kropotkin zum Studium aus:
*System der gegenseitigen Hilfe
in der Natur.* Ein schwacher Trost.

Wir haben mit Bedauern vernommen,
daß es keine Gerechtigkeit gibt,
und mit noch größerem Bedauern,
daß es, wie die bewußten Kreise
händereibend versichern, auch nichts
dergleichen je geben kann, soll und wird.

Strittig ist nach wie vor, wer oder was
daran schuld sei. Ist es die Erbsünde
oder die Genetik? die Säuglingspflege?
der Mangel an Herzensbildung?
die falsche Diät? der Gottseibeiuns?
die Männerherrschaft? das Kapital?

Cold Comfort

Man's struggle against man,
according to reliable sources
close to the Home Office,
will be nationalised in due course,
down to the last bloodstain.
Kind regards from Thomas Hobbes.

A civil war fought with unequal arms:
one man's tax return
is another man's bicycle chain.
Poisoners and incendiaries
are planning to form a union
and call for job protection.

Our prison service
is utterly open-minded.
They offer Kropotkin's *System
of Mutual Aid in the Natural World*,
bound in washable black plastic covers,
as a study course. This is cold comfort.

We have learned to our dismay
that there is no justice,
and furthermore, to our even greater dismay,
from informed sources beaming with satisfaction,
that nothing remotely like it
can, should or will ever exist.

It is not yet quite clear
whose fault this may be. Original Sin?
Genetics? Methods of infant care?
The lack of polite education?
Capitalism? Unhealthy diet?
The Devil? Or Male Domination?

Daß wir es leider nicht lassen können,
einander zu notzüchtigen,
an die nächstbeste Kreuzung zu nageln
und die Überreste zu essen, schön wär es,
dafür eine Erklärung zu finden,
Balsam für die Vernunft.

Zwar die tägliche Scheußlichkeit stört,
doch sie wundert uns wenig.
Was aber rätselhaft anmutet, ist
die stille Handreichung,
die grundlose Gutmütigkeit,
sowie die englische Sanftmut.

Also höchste Zeit, mit feuriger Zunge
den Kellner zu loben, der stundenlang
der Tirade des Impotenten lauscht;
den Barmherzigkeit übenden Knäckebrot-
Vertreter, der kurz vor dem tödlichen Schlag
den Zahlungsbefehl sinken läßt;

wie auch die Betschwester, die,
unverhofft, den atemlos an ihre Tür
hämmernden Deserteur versteckt;
und den Entführer, der sein wirres Werk
mit einem matten, zufriedenen Lächeln
unversehens aufgibt, zu Tode erschöpft;

und wir legen die Zeitung weg
und freuen uns, achselzuckend, so,
wie wenn der Schmachtfetzen glücklich aus ist,
wenn es hell wird im Kino, und draußen
hat es zu regnen aufgehört, dann blüht uns
endlich der erste Zug aus der Zigarette.

Unfortunately we cannot refrain
from rape and from ravishment,
from nailing each other down
to the nearest crosswalk
and from gobbling up the remains.
To find out why would be nice,
balm on the wounds of Reason.

We are annoyed but not surprised
by our daily atrocities.
What we find puzzling
are mild ministrations,
groundless generosity
and angelical sweetness.

It is therefore high time
to praise with fiery tongues
the waiter listening for hours on end
to the impotent man's lamentation:
the biscuit salesman showing mercy
and tearing up at the last moment
the writ of execution;

the bigoted spinster hiding,
strangely enough, the deserter
hammering breathlessly at her door;
and the kidnapper, suddenly tired
to death, giving up his tangled work
with a feeble, contented smile.

With a shrug we put the newspaper down,
filled with joy, the kind of joy
we feel when the B-picture
finally draws to an end, the lights
come on in the cinema, outside
the rain has stopped, and we long
for our first puff of smoke.

Weitere Gründe dafür, daß die Dichter lügen

Weil der Augenblick,
in dem das Wort *glücklich*
ausgesprochen wird,
niemals der glückliche Augenblick ist.
Weil der Verdurstende seinen Durst
nicht über die Lippen bringt.
Weil im Munde der Arbeiterklasse
das Wort *Arbeiterklasse* nicht vorkommt.
Weil, wer verzweifelt,
nicht Lust hat, zu sagen:
»Ich bin ein Verzweifelnder.«
Weil Orgasmus und *Orgasmus*
nicht miteinander vereinbar sind.
Weil der Sterbende, statt zu behaupten:
»Ich sterbe jetzt«,
nur ein mattes Geräusch vernehmen läßt,
das wir nicht verstehen.
Weil es die Lebenden sind,
die den Toten in den Ohren liegen
mit ihren Schreckensnachrichten.
Weil die Wörter zu spät kommen,
oder zu früh.
Weil es also ein anderer ist,
immer ein anderer,
der da redet,
und weil der,
von dem da die Rede ist,
schweigt.

Further Reasons Why Poets Do Not Tell the Truth

Because the moment
when the word *happy*
is pronounced
never is the moment of happiness.
Because the thirsty man
does not give mouth to his thirst.
Because *proletariat* is a word
which will not pass the lips of the proletariat.
Because he who despairs
does not feel like saying:
'I am desperate.'
Because orgasm and *orgasm*
are worlds apart.
Because the dying man,
far from proclaiming:
'I die,' only utters
a faint rattle,
which we fail to comprehend.
Because it is the living
who batter the ears of the dead
with their atrocities.
Because words come always
too late or too soon.
Because it is someone else,
always someone else,
who does the talking,
and because he
who is being talked about,
keeps his silence.

Nur die Ruhe

Zuweilen, wenn auch nicht oft, sieht man im Schnee,
bei winterlichen Hasenjagden, oder, kurz vor Ostern,
durch das halb geöffnete Schlafwagenfenster,
während es hell wird draußen, auf Scheunendächern,
Kohlenhalden, Bismarcktürmen im Mischwald,
kleine Schwärme von schwarz gekleideten Leuten,
angeführt von einem Propheten, die Nickelbrille
auf den geblähten Nüstern, unbeweglich verharren
in Erwartung des Weltunterganges. Während wir andern,
beschäftigt mit unsern wichtigen Kinkerlitzchen,
die Sintflut im fernsten Perfekt vermuten,
oder wir halten sie gar für eine ehrwürdige Ente,
wissen jene, im Hochsitz lauernd, auf die Minute genau,
Wann. Rechtzeitig haben sie ihre Fernseher abgemeldet,
den Kühlschrank ausgeräumt, damit nichts verdirbt,
und ihre Seele gerüstet. Erschütternd dünn
wehn uns ihre Stimmchen ins Ohr über die bereinigte Flur,
den Ruhrschnellweg, den kühlen, baureifen Wiesengrund:
Näher, mein Gott, zu Dir. Auf die Dauer freilich
wird es kaum zu vermeiden sein, daß der eine
oder der andere auf die Uhr blickt und stutzt;
daß dem Propheten der mahnend erhobene Arm lahmt;
und daß, während es aufklart, der D-Zug vorbeirappelt,
die Halden schrumpfen, der Schnee schmilzt
und die Hasen in die Bratröhre wandern, einer
nach dem andern sich, unter dem höhnischen Beifall
der Mitwelt, wieder abseilen wird in den niederen Alltag,
das Gehaltkonto neu eröffnen, eine Gießkanne kaufen,
sich gefaßt machen auf den unvermeidlichen Urlaub.
Angesichts der Allgemeinen Geschäftsbedingungen
und der schmutzigen Wäsche muß sogar der Prophet
gewisse Zugeständnisse machen, aber hart bleibt er
in der Sache. Mit dünner doch fester Stimme sagt er sich:
Das sind alles Äußerlichkeiten. Nur Geduld!
Ein paar Wochen oder Jahrhunderte hin oder her,
was verschlägt das schon im Vergleich mit der Ewigkeit.

Keeping Cool

Sometimes, not very frequently, hunting hares in the winter,
you will perceive in the snow, or shortly before Easter,
peering through the half-open window of your sleeping car,
against the dawning day, on the roof of a lonely barn,
on a pile of coal, or on a belvedere across the valley,
a small flock of people dressed in black coats,
led by a prophet with steel-rimmed spectacles
and flared nostrils, motionless, silent, waiting
for Doom to come. We, of course, go on bothering
about our humdrum business, supposing the deluge
to be something antediluvian, or else
an elaborate practical joke—while they, perched
on their respective lookouts, know exactly the moment
When. They have returned their hired cars in good time,
emptied their fridges and prepared their souls.
Terribly thin is the sound of their voices,
swept by the wind across the freeway, the shady dell
due for development: 'Nearer, my god, to Thee.'
In the long run, however, it can hardly be helped
that first one, then another will glance at his watch
and be taken aback; the prophet's arm, raised in admonition,
will go to sleep; and while the weak sun rises,
the train passes by, the coal is burnt up,
the snow melts away and the hares end up in the oven,
first one, then another will slowly come down
and join us in the nether regions of routine,
meeting the mockery of the commonplace,
buying a toothbrush, reopening his bank account
and bracing himself for the inevitable holidays.
Even the prophet himself, faced with the small print
and with dirty linen, will have to make allowances,
hanging on, however, to the essentials.
His voice may crack but it does not fail him.
Outward appearances do not matter. What are weeks
or even centuries, compared to Eternity?

Was ihn betrifft, er wird, wenn es einst soweit ist,
keineswegs überrascht sein. Von jeher schließlich
hat er sich auf den Standpunkt gestellt: So
kann es nicht weitergehen! Recht werde uns geschehen!
Selber schuld! Hätten wir nur beizeiten auf ihn gehört!
Und also fühlt er auf seinem Scheunendach, unverzagt
krähend, daß der Weltuntergang immer aufs neue,
und wäre er noch so unpünktlich, mundet wie Manna,
daß er eine Art von Beruhigung ist, ein süßer Trost
bei trüber Aussicht, bei Haarausfall, und bei nassen Füßen.

He for his part will not be surprised
by the Day of Reckoning. I told you so, he will mutter.
Things just couldn't go on like this. But unfortunately
nobody listened to me. And thus even now he feels,
perched on the top of his barn and crowing away,
that Doom, however unpunctual, will always be
a tranquilliser of sorts, a sweet consolation
for dull prospects, loss of hair, and wet feet.

Erkenntnistheoretisches Modell

Hier hast du
eine große Schachtel
mit der Aufschrift
Schachtel.
Wenn du sie öffnest,
findest du darin
eine Schachtel
mit der Aufschrift
Schachtel
aus einer Schachtel
mit der Aufschrift
Schachtel.
Wenn du sie öffnest—
ich meine jetzt
diese Schachtel,
nicht jene—,
findest du darin
eine Schachtel
mit der Aufschrift
Und so weiter,
und wenn du
so weiter machst,
findest du
nach unendlichen Mühen
eine unendlich kleine
Schachtel
mit einer Aufschrift
so winzig,
daß sie dir gleichsam
vor den Augen
verdunstet.
Es ist eine Schachtel,
die nur in deiner Einbildung
existiert.
Eine vollkommen leere
Schachtel.

Model toward a Theory of Cognition

Here is a box for you,
a large box
labelled
Box.
Open it,
and you will find
a box in it,
labelled
Box from a box
labelled Box.
Look into it
(I mean this box now,
not the other one),
and you will find a box
labelled
And so on,
and if you go on
like this,
you will find,
after infinite efforts,
an infinitely small
box
with a label
so tiny
that the lettering,
as it were,
dissolves
before your eyes.
It is a box
existing only
in your imagination.
A perfectly empty
box.

Erkennungsdienstliche Behandlung

Das ist nicht Dante.
Das ist eine Photographie von Dante.
Das ist ein Film, in dem ein Schauspieler auftritt, der vorgibt,
       Dante zu sein.
Das ist ein Film, in dem Dante Dante spielt.
Das ist ein Mann, der von Dante träumt.
Das ist ein Mann, der Dante heißt, aber nicht Dante ist.
Das ist ein Mann, der Dante nachäfft.
Das ist ein Mann, der sich für Dante ausgibt.
Das ist ein Mann, der träumt, er sei Dante.
Das ist ein Mann, der Dante zum Verwechseln ähnlich sieht.
Das ist eine Wachsfigur von Dante.
Das ist ein Wechselbalg, ein Zwilling, ein Doppelgänger.
Das ist ein Mann, der sich für Dante hält.
Das ist ein Mann, den alle, außer Dante, für Dante halten.
Das ist ein Mann, den alle für Dante halten, nur er selber glaubt
       nicht daran.
Das ist ein Mann, den niemand für Dante hält außer Dante.
Das ist Dante.

Identity Check

This is not Dante.
This is a photograph of Dante.
This is a film showing an actor who pretends to be Dante.
This is a film with Dante in the role of Dante.
This is a man who dreams of Dante.
This is a man called Dante who is not Dante.
This is a man who apes Dante.
This is a man who passes himself off as Dante.
This is a man who dreams that he is Dante.
This is a man who is the very spit image of Dante.
This is a wax figure of Dante.
This is a changeling, a double, an identical twin.
This is a man who believes he is Dante.
This is a man everybody, except Dante, believes to be Dante.
This is a man everybody believes to be Dante, only he himself
        does not fall for it.
This is a man nobody believes to be Dante, except Dante.
This is Dante.

Forschungsgemeinschaft

O Propheten mit dem Rücken zum Meer,
mit dem Rücken zur Gegenwart, o seelenruhig
in die Zukunft blickende Zauberkünstler,
o immerfort an die Reling gelehnte Schamanen—
einmal ein Taschenbuch durchgeblättert,
das genügt, um euch zu begreifen!

Aus Knochen lesen, aus Sternen, aus Scherben,
zum Wohle der Allgemeinheit, aus Eingeweiden,
was gewesen ist und was bevorsteht—
O Wissenschaft! Gebenedeit seist du,
gebenedeit deine kleinen Lichtblicke,
halb Bluff halb Statistik: Todesarten,
Geldmengenziele, wachsende Entropie…

Weiter so! Diese schwefelgelben Erleuchtungen
sind besser als nichts, sie unterhalten uns
an dunstigen Sommerabenden:
Papierbahnen frisch vom Computer,
Stichproben, Ausgrabungen, Tips
nach der Delphi-Methode—bravo!

Gebenedeit sei das Vorläufige!
Vorläufig ist noch genug frisches Wasser da,
vorläufig atmet und lauscht die Haut,
deine Haut, meine,—sogar die eure,
ihr holzigen Medizinmänner, atmet noch,
ungeachtet der Bleibeverhandlungen,
der Fußnoten und des Stellenkegels—
vorläufig ist das Ende (»eine unaufhörliche,
feinverteilte Naturkatastrophe«)
noch nicht endgültig—das ist angenehm!

Also am Wochenende, liebe Mitwisser,
—vor Neufundland vereinzelt Eisberge,
über Mitteleuropa Sommergewitter,
schweflig am dunstigen Horizont—
nichts wie raus aus den Instituten!

Research Council

O prophets with your backs turned to the sea,
with your backs turned to the present, O sorcerers
looking placidly into the future,
O shaman priests forever leaning over the railing—
one single paperback leafed through
is enough to see through your mysteries!

Reading in bones, in stars, in debris,
from entrails, all that has been and all
that is bound to happen, for the public good,
O Science! be blessed and blessed be
the rather minor rays of light which you offer us,
half bluff and half statistics: mortalities,
money supply targets, increasing entropy...

Carry on! All these brimstone-coloured illuminations
are better than nothing at all,
they keep us happy on sultry summer nights:
computer print-outs fresh from the backroom,
sample probes, excavations, tip-offs
based on the Delphi method—hear, hear!

Blessed be your interim reports!
For the time being there is enough fresh water left,
the skin is still breathing expectantly,
my skin twitches, our skin, and even yours,
you dead-alive medicine men,
notwithstanding the question of tenure,
the footnotes and the likelihood of advancement—
for the time being the end (an interminable,
finely scattered act of God)
is not yet final—a comforting thought!

And hence, my dear accessories before the fact,
while off Newfoundland icebergs are being forecast
and thunderstorms in the sulphur-lined skies
of Central Europe, you had better get out
of your institutes for the weekend. Run

Ein bißchen Leben am Wochenende,
was immer das heißen mag, vorläufig
natürlich nur, und ohne prognostischen Wert.

O ihr ewig nach Erkenntnissen Dürstenden,
ihr dauert mich, wie ihr dann auf der Datscha.
im irischen Bauernhaus, auf Korčula,
mit dem Rücken zum Meer, seelenruhig
euer Gehirn ausklinkt—daß euch allerdings
beim Ping-Pong die Fackel nicht ausgehe!
Nur so weiter! Ich segne euch.

for your life, or a slice of it, an interim,
whatever that may mean, until Monday;
though as a basis for your predictions
this course of action may not be much good.

O my friends, ever thirsting for knowledge,
I pity you, resting at your dachas,
your Irish cottages, or in Korčula,
turning your backs on the sea
and switching your brains off, placidly.
Onward, and may your torch never go out
during the ping-pong match! I bless you.

Fachschaft Philosophie

Daß wir gescheit sind, ist wahr. Aber weit entfernt,
die Welt zu verändern, ziehen wir auf dem Podium
Kaninchen aus unserm Gehirn, Kaninchen und Tauben,
Schwärme von schneeweißen Tauben, die unverwandt
auf die Bücher kacken. Daß Vernunft Vernunft ist
und nicht Vernunft, um das zu kapieren,
braucht man nicht Hegel zu sein, dazu genügt
ein Blick in den Taschenspiegel. Er zeigt uns
in wallenden blauen Mäntelchen, bestickt
mit silbernen Sternen, und auf dem Kopf
einen spitzen Hut. Im Keller versammeln wir uns,
wo die Karteileichen liegen, zum Hegelkongreß,
packen unsre Kristallkugeln und Horoskope aus
und machen uns an die Arbeit. Gutachten
schwenken wir, Pendel, Forschungsberichte,
wir lassen die Tische rücken, wir fragen:
Wie wirklich ist das, was wirklich ist? Schadenfroh
lächelt Hegel. Wir malen ihm einen Schnurrbart an.
Schon sieht er wie Stalin aus. Der Kongreß
tanzt. Weit und breit kein Vulkan. Unauffällig
stehen die Posten Posten. In aller Ruhe wirft,
Knüppel aus dem Sack, unser psychischer Apparat
treffende Sätze aus, und wir sagen uns:
In jedem brutalen Bullen steckt doch
ein verständnisvoller Helfer und Freund,
in dem ein brutaler Bulle steckt. Simsalabim!
Wie ein enormes Taschentuch entfalten wir
die Theorie, während vor dem verbunkerten Seminar
bescheiden die Herren im Trenchcoat warten.
Sie rauchen, machen kaum Gebrauch von der Dienstwaffe,
und bewachen die Planstellen, die Papierblumen
und den schneeweiß alles bedeckenden Taubendreck.

Dept. of Philosophy

No doubt we are intelligent. But far
from changing the face of the world, on stage
we keep producing rabbits from our brains
and snow-white pigeons, swarms of pigeons
who invariably shit on the books.
You don't have to be Hegel to catch on to the fact
that Reason is both reasonable and against Reason.
All it takes is a look into your pocket mirror.
You will see yourself wearing a blue gown,
spangled with silver stars, and a pointed hat.
For the Hegel Congress we meet in the cellar
where our card-file colleagues are buried,
unpack our crystal balls and our horoscopes,
and go to work, waving our expertise,
our pendulum and our research reports.
We make the tables turn, we ask reality
How real is it? Hegel is smiling,
filled with *schadenfreude.* We daub his face
with an inky moustache. He now looks like Stalin.
The congress is having a ball, but there is
no volcano in sight to dance on. The guards
outside are on their guard. Our pysche
calmly produces pertinent statements,
and we agree that deep down in any given brutal pig
a well-meaning public servant is to be found
and the other way round. Abracadabra!
Like an enormous handkerchief we unfold
our theories. The plainclothes men
in their trench coats are modestly waiting
in front of the riot-proof seminar shelter.
They smoke, they hardly ever make use of their guns,
they keep guard on our faculty roster, our paper flowers
and the snow-white pigeon droppings all over the place.

Die Ruhe auf der Flucht. Flämisch, 1521

Ich sehe das spielende Kind im Korn,
das den Bären nicht sieht.
Der Bär umarmt oder schlägt einen Bauern.
Den Bauern sieht er,
aber er sieht das Messer nicht,
das in seinem Rücken steckt;
nämlich im Rücken des Bären.

Auf dem Hügel drüben liegen die Überreste
eines Geräderten; doch der Spielmann,
der vorübergeht, weiß nichts davon.
Auch bemerken die beiden Heere,
die auf der hell erleuchteten Ebene
gegeneinander vorrücken—
ihre Lanzen funkeln und blenden mich—,
den kreisenden Sperber nicht,
der sie ins kalte Auge faßt.

Ich sehe deutlich die Schimmelfäden,
die sich durch das Dachgebälk ziehen,
im Vordergrund, und weiter hinten
den vorbeisprengenden Kurier.
Aus einem Hohlweg muß er aufgetaucht sein.
Niemals werde ich wissen,
wie dieser Hohlweg von innen aussieht;
aber ich denke mir,
daß er feucht ist, schattig und feucht.

Die Schwäne auf dem Teich in der Mitte des Bildes
nehmen keine Notiz von mir.
Ich betrachte den Tempel am Abgrund,
den schwarzen Elefanten—seltsam,
ein schwarzer Elefant auf freiem Feld!—
und die Statuen, deren weiße Augen
dem Vogelfänger im Wald zusehen,
dem Fährmann, der Feuersbrunst.
Wie lautlos das alles ist!

The Rest on the Flight. Flemish, 1521

I see the child playing in the corn,
who does not see the bear.
I see the bear hugging or killing a peasant.
He sees the peasant,
but not the knife
sticking in his back,
that is, in the back of the bear.

On the hill over there lie the remains
of a man who was put to the wheel;
but the minstrel passing by
does not notice them.
As for the two legions
advancing upon each other
on the brightly lit plain,
the flash of their lances is blinding me,
but they fail to observe the hawk circling overhead
who keeps a cold eye on them.

I distinguish the threads of mould
dangling from the roof beam
in the foreground, and in the distance
I perceive the courier galloping by.
He must have emerged from a ravine.
Never shall I come to know
what this ravine looks like from within;
but I imagine that it is damp,
very damp, and full of shadows.

To the centre of the picture the swans
in the pond ignore me.
I see the temple on the edge of the precipice,
the black elephant on guard
(how strange to see a black elephant in the open fields!)
and the statues, who out of their white eyes
watch the fowler in the forest,
the ferryman, and the conflagration.
How silently all these things come to pass!

Auf sehr entlegenen, sehr hohen Türmen
mit fremdartigen Schießscharten
seh ich die Eulen zwinkern. Ja,
dies alles sehe ich wohl,
doch worauf es ankommt, das weiß ich nicht.
Wie sollte ich es erraten,
da alles das, was ich sehe,
so deutlich ist, so notwendig
und so undurchdringlich?

Nichts ahnend, in meine Geschäfte versunken
wie in die ihrigen jene Stadt,
oder wie weit in der Ferne
jene noch viel blaueren Städte
verschwimmend in andern Erscheinungen,
andern Wolken, Heeren und Ungeheuern,
lebe ich weiter. Ich gehe fort.
Ich habe dies alles gesehen, nur
das Messer, das mir im Rücken steckt, nicht.

On very remote, lofty towers
with uncommon embrasures
I see the owls winking. O yes,
all these things I can well see,
but how should I know what matters
and what does not? How should I guess?
Everything here seems evident,
equally distinct, necessary
and impenetrable.

Out of my depth, lost in my own concerns,
just like the faraway city over there,
and like those other cities, even bluer
and even more distant,
dissolving into other visions,
other clouds, legions and monsters,
I go on living. I go away.
I have seen all this, but I cannot see
the knife sticking in my back.

THE FURY OF DISAPPEARANCE

DIE FURIE DES VERSCHWINDENS

(1980)

Die Dreiunddreißigjährige

Sie hat sich das alles ganz anders vorgestellt.
Immer diese verrosteten Volkswagen.
Einmal hätte sie fast einen Bäcker geheiratet.
Erst hat sie Hesse gelesen, dann Handke.
Jetzt löst sie öfter Silbenrätsel im Bett.
Von Männern läßt sie sich nichts gefallen.
Jahrelang war sie Trotzkistin, aber auf ihre Art.
Sie hat nie eine Brotmarke in der Hand gehabt.
Wenn sie an Kambodscha denkt, wird ihr ganz schlecht.
Ihr letzter Freund, der Professor, wollte immer verhaut werden.
Grünliche Batik-Kleider, die ihr zu weit sind.
Blattläuse auf der Zimmerlinde.
Eigentlich wollte sie malen, oder auswandern.
Ihre Dissertation, *Klassenkämpfe in Ulm, 1500
bis 1512, und ihre Spuren im Volkslied:*
Stipendien, Anfänge und ein Koffer voller Notizen.
Manchmal schickt ihr die Großmutter Geld.
Zaghafte Tänze im Badezimmer, kleine Grimassen,
stundenlang Gurkenmilch vor dem Spiegel.
Sie sagt: Ich werde schon nicht verhungern.
Wenn sie weint, sieht sie aus wie neunzehn.

At Thirty-Three

It was all so different from what she'd expected.
Always those rusting Volkswagens.
At one time she'd almost married a baker.
First she read Hesse, then Handke.
Now often she does crosswords in bed.
With her, men take no liberties.
For years she was a Trotskyist, but in her own way.
She's never handled a ration card.
When she thinks of Kampuchea she feels quite sick.
Her last lover, the professor, always wanted her to beat him.
Greenish batik dresses, always too wide for her.
Greenflies on her *Sparmannia*.
Really she wanted to paint, or emigrate.
Her thesis, *Class Struggles in Ulm 1500*
to 1512 and References to them in Folksong:
Grants, beginnings and a suitcase full of notes.
Sometimes her grandmother sends her money.
Tentative dances in her bathroom, little grimaces,
cucumber juice for hours in front of the mirror.
She says, whatever happens I shan't starve.
When she weeps she looks like nineteen.

Der Angestellte

Nie hat et jemanden umgebracht. Nein,
er wirft aus Versehen Flaschen um.
Er möchte gern, schwitzt, verliert
seinen liebsten Schlüssel. Immerzu
erkältet er sich. Er weiß, daß er muß.
Er mutet sich Mut zu, er gähnt,
er tupft seinen Gram auf den Putz.
Er denkt, lieber nicht. Eingezwängt
in zwei Schuhe, beteuert er bleich
das Gegenteil. Ja, er meldet sich an
und ab. Das Gegenteil sagt er von dem,
was er sagen wollte. Eigentlich, sagt er,
eigentlich nicht. Der Anzug ist ihm zu eng,
zu weit. Seine Stelle schmerzt. Nein,
seine eigene Handschrift kann er schon längst
nicht mehr lesen. Er hat sich scheiden lassen,
vergebens. Kein Mensch ruft ihn an. Überall
juckt es ihn. Sein Kugelschreiber läuft aus,
beim besten Willen. Er ist öfters vorhanden,
in jedem Zimmer einmal, immer allein.
Er schneidet sich beim Rasieren. Ja,
er paßt nämlich immer auf, sonst
kann er nicht schlafen. Er schläft.
Alles meckert, alles was recht ist,
alles lacht über ihn. Er merkt nicht,
was los ist. Das merkt er. Sein Kopfweh
ist unpolitisch. Er stellt sich an,
er stottert schon wieder, verschluckt sich.
Was er vorhin hat sagen wollen, das hat er
vorhin vergessen. Er hat vergessen,
sich umzubringen. Beim besten Willen.
Heimlich lebt er. Nein, er darf nicht,
aber er müßte. Er hat keinen Krebs,
aber das weiß er nicht. Sein Hut schwitzt.
Es ist ihm noch nie so gut gegangen
wie jetzt. Eigentlich möchte er nicht,
aber er muß. Er weint beim Friseur. Ja,
er ist anstellig, er entschuldigt sich.

146

The Employee

He has never killed anyone. No,
he upsets bottles by accident.
He would like to, sweats, loses
his favourite key. All the time
he catches colds. He knows that he must.
He supposes he could be brave, he yawns,
he dabs his grief on to the stucco.
He thinks, better not. Jammed into
a pair of shoes, palely he asserts
the opposite. Yes, he reports himself in
and out. He says the opposite of
what he wanted to say. Really, he says,
really not. His suit is too tight for him,
too wide. His place hurts. No,
for a long time he has been unable
to read his own handwriting. He divorced,
in vain. No one rings him up. He itches
all over. His ball-pen runs out,
with the best will. He is often present,
once in each room, always alone.
He cuts himself shaving. Yes,
for he always takes care, otherwise
he can't sleep. He sleeps.
Everyone cackles, everyone who is right,
everyone laughs at him. He can't see
what's wrong. He sees it all right. His headache
is unpolitical. He tries hard,
he's stammering again, begins to choke.
What he wanted to say a moment ago, he
forgot a moment ago. He has forgotten
to do away with himself. With the best will.
Secretly he lives. No, he must not,
but he ought to. He doesn't have cancer
but he doesn't know that. His hat sweats.
He has never done as well
as he's doing now. Really, he'd rather not,
but he must. He weeps at the hairdresser's. Yes,
he's efficient enough, he apologises.

Ja, er schreibt, ja, er kratzt sich,
ja, er müßte, aber er darf nicht,
nein, seinen Jammer hat niemand bemerkt.

Yes, he writes, yes, he scratches himself.
Yes, he ought to, but he mustn't.
No, his misery has not been noticed by anyone.

Die Scheidung

Erst war es nur ein unmerkliches Beben der Haut—
»Wie du meinst«—, dort wo das Fleisch am dunkelsten ist.
»Was hast du?«—Nichts. Milchige Träume
von Umarmungen, aber am anderen Morgen
sieht der andere anders aus, sonderbar knochig.
Messerscharfe Mißverständnisse. »Damals in Rom—«
Das habe ich nie gesagt.—Pause. Rasendes Herzklopfen,
eine Art Haß, sonderbar.—»Darum geht es nicht.«
Wiederholungen. Strahlend hell die Gewißheit:
Von nun an ist alles falsch. Geruchlos und scharf,
wie ein Paßfoto, diese unbekannte Person
mit dem Teeglas am Tisch, mit starren Augen.
Es hat keinen Zweck keinen Zweck keinen Zweck:
Litanei im Kopf, ein Anflug von Übelkeit.
Ende der Vorwürfe. Langsam füllt sich
das ganze Zimmer bis zur Decke mit Schuld.
Die klagende Stimme ist fremd, nur die Schuhe,
die krachend zu Boden fallen, die Schuhe nicht.
Das nächste Mal, in einem leeren Restaurant,
Zeitlupe, Brotbrösel, wird über Geld gesprochen,
lachend. Der Nachtisch schmeckt nach Metall.
Zwei Unberührbare. Schrille Vernunft.
»Alles halb so schlimm.« Aber nachts
die Rachsucht, der stumme Kampf, anonym,
wie zwei knochige Advokaten, zwei große Krebse
im Wasser. Dann die Erschöpfung. Langsam
blättert der Schorf ab. Ein neues Tabakgeschäft,
eine neue Adresse. Parias, schrecklich erleichtert.
Blasser werdende Schatten. Dies sind die Akten.
Dies ist der Schlüsselbund. Dies ist die Narbe.

The Divorce

At first it was only an imperceptible quivering of the skin—
'As you wish'—where the flesh is darkest.
'What's wrong with you?'—Nothing. Milky dreams
of embraces; next morning, though,
the other looks different, strangely bony.
Razor-sharp misunderstandings. 'That time, in Rome—'
I never said that. A pause. And furious palpitations,
a sort of hatred, strange. 'That's not the point.'
Repetitions. Radiantly clear, this certainty:
From now on all is wrong. Odourless and sharp,
like a passport photo, this unknown person
with a glass of tea at table, with staring eyes.
It's no good, no good, no good:
litany in the head, a slight nausea.
End of reproaches. Slowly the whole room
fills with guilt right up to the ceiling.
This complaining voice is strange, only not
the shoes that drop with a bang, not the shoes.
Next time, in an empty restaurant
slow motion, bread crumbs, money is discussed,
laughing. The dessert tastes of metal.
Two untouchables. Shrill reasonableness.
'Not so bad really.' But at night
the thoughts of vengeance, the silent fight, anonymous
like two bony barristers, two large crabs
in water. Then the exhaustion. Slowly
the scab peels off. A new tobacconist,
a new address. Pariahs, horribly relieved.
Shades growing paler. These are the documents.
This is the bunch of keys. This is the scar.

Der Urlaub

Jetzt, wo er frei hat, verhältnismäßig, schlurft er
oft um die Tennisplätze, läßt sich rasieren, liest.
Schwarzhändler wispern, Turnschuhe hecheln vorbei.
Starrend vor Palmen dehnt sich die Welt
am Sonntag. Im Palace brüten die ersten Huren
über dem Frühstück. Alles klar, alles fusselt.
Menschenskind, Mecki, ruft es vom Nebentisch.
Heulendes Elend am Strand. Umständehalber
schmelzen Peseten. Zufallsbekanntschaften,
sehnsüchtig eingekremt. »Was sagst du dazu, José,
wenn ich heut nacht mit dir geh? Olé, olé, olé.«
Ekelhaft, dieser Tintenfisch auf dem Teller.
Das gähnende Zimmer. Sand in den Handtüchern.
Ein helles Insekt, das sich gegen die Birne wirft.
Siebzehn senkrecht: Griechische Fruchtbarkeitsgöttin.
Die Dusche riecht muffig. Auf der Straße kichert es.
Motorräder starten. Dann ist nur noch das Meer da,
das in der Ferne ächzt. Nein, nebenan ist es,
nebenenan stirbt eine Frau oder liebt sich selbst.
Olé, olé, was sagst du dazu, José? Er horcht.
Weiß im Zahnputzglas wimmeln die Schlaftabletten.

The Holiday

Now that he's free, relatively, often he shuffles
round the tennis courts, pays for a shave, reads.
Black marketeers whisper, plimsolls pant past him.
Stiff with palm trees, the world expands
on Sundays. Here, in the Palace, the first whores
brood over their breakfast. All is clear, all fuzzes.
Well, if it isn't Nick! comes from the next table.
On the beach, howling misery. Complications
melt away pesetas. Chance acquaintances,
longingly primed with lotion. 'What do you say, José,
if tonight we go and play? Olé, olé, olé.'
Disgusting, this octopus on the plate.
The yawning bedroom. Sand in the towels.
A brilliant insect that collides with the lighbulb.
At seventeen degrees: Greek fertility goddess.
The shower smells musty. In the street someone titters.
Motorbikes rev. Then there's only the sea
that sighs away into the distance. No, it's the next room,
in the next room a woman is dying or loving herself.
Olé, olé what do you say, José? He listens.
White in his tooth-glass the sleeping tablets teem.

Ein Treppenhaus

Wenn du nach Dublin kommst, sagte sie damals,
die Adresse hast du ja. Also sitze ich hier
auf der letzten Stufe, unter dem Dach,
im Halbdunkel, ab und zu hallen Schritte
von unten her, klackende Hacken, dann
schlägt eine Tür mit grünem Filz
an die Wand geschrieben: *Komme gleich wieder,*
mit Lipenstift: *Molly war da. Ruf mich an,*
und unter dem abgerissenen Klingeldraht
eine Telefonnummer. Wie viele Jahre lang
wird das noch alles da stehen, die Wörter,
die Wände? Niemand kommt. Und ich frage mich,
wie sie aussah. Nur was mich störte,
das weiß ich noch: ihr elektrisches Zappeln,
der Jodgeruch, das Gelb im Weiß ihrer Augen,
die Puderflecken, das alte Feldbett und später
das Heulen des Teekessels auf dem Herd.
Eine Fremde. Ich rühre mich nicht.
Am liebsten bliebe ich hier, summend,
im Treppenhaus, bis der Bulldozer kommt.

A Staircase

If you're in Dublin, she said that time,
you have the address. So I'm sitting here
on the top stair, under the roof,
in half-light; from time to time I can hear
footsteps below, heels clacking, then
a door slams, silence. Drowsy,
with the help of a lighter, I read
this message scrawled on the wall,
with a green felt pen, near the frame
of the cracked door: *Back very soon*,
with an eye pencil: *Molly was here. Ring me*,
and under the ripped-out doorbell wire
a telephone number. How many more years
are they likely to last, the messages,
the walls? No one comes. And I try to recall
what she looked like. All I remember
is the things I disliked: her electric twitch,
the iodine smell, the yellow in the white of her eyes,
the blotches of powder, the old camp bed and, later,
the howling of her kettle on the stove.
A stranger. I do not stir.
What I'd like best is to stay here, humming
on the staircase, till the bulldozer comes.

Stadtrundfahrt

Da drüben kauert der Schuhputzer,
der keine Schuhe mehr braucht;
denn seine Beine sind verfault
im Fernen Osten vor langer Zeit.

Das ist der Rauch von den Werften.

Dieses Café war früher ganz schwarz
von Hausierern und armen Dichtern.
Spitzel wie Mücken saßen dort
und tranken aus kleinen Tassen Blut.

Hier gibt es weiche Mädchen
gegen harte Devisen.
Das Pflaster ist aufgerissen.
Dort standen damals die Panzer.

Da ist im Sommer immer
der Kaiser spazierengefahren—
Stadtwäldchenallee, heute Gorkij fasor.
Das ist das Zentralkomitee.

Das ist der Rauch von den Schlachthöfen.

Hier ist mein Freund Sandór geboren
vor dem Zweiten Weltkrieg,
in der Beletage,
wo es Tag und Nacht dunkel war.

Siehst du den Rauch?

Diese Brücke war ganz zerstört.
Hier trinken die reichen Dichter Tee
und schimpfen leise,
und dort wird das neue Hilton gebaut.

Sightseeing Tour

Over there the old shoe-shine boy
who can do without shoes,
for his legs rotted away
in the Far East a long time ago.

This is the smoke from the ship-yards.

This café used to be packed
with hawkers and penniless poets.
Informers descended like mosquitoes
and drank blood from little cups.

Here there are soft girls on sale
for hard currency.
The pavement is torn up.
This is where the tanks came in.

Here the Emperor went for his drive
in the summertime, every day—
Stadtwäldchenallee, today Gorkij fasor.
This is the Central Committee.

That is the smoke from the stockyards.

Here my friend Sandór was born
before the Second World War
on the first floor
where the daylight never came in.

Do you see the smoke?

The bridge over there was completely destroyed.
Here the well-to-do poets take their tea
grumbling softly,
and there the new Hilton is going up.

Auf dieser wackligen Parkbank
sitzt manchmal ein alter Mann,
der manchmal die Wahrheit sagt.
Heute ist er nicht da.

Aber der Rauch. Siehst du den Rauch,

den alten Rauch über Budapest?

On this rickety park-bench
an old man can sometimes be seen
who sometimes tells the truth.
He did not show up today.

But the smoke. Do you see the smoke

the old smoke over Budapest?

Kurze Geschichte der Bourgeoisie

Dies war der Augenblick, da wir,
ohne es zu bemerken, fünf Minuten lang
unermeßlich reich waren, großzügig
und elektrisch, gekühlt im Juli,
oder für den Fall daß es November war,
loderte das eingeflogene finnische Holz
in den Renaissancekaminen. Komisch,
alles war da, flog sich ein,
gewissermaßen von selber. Elegant
waren wir, niemand konnte uns leiden.
Wir warfen um uns mit Solokonzerten,
Chips, Orchideen in Cellophan. Wolken,
die Ich sagten. Einmalig!

Überallhin Linienflüge. Selbst unsre Seufzer
gingen auf Scheckkarte. Wie die Rohrspatzen
schimpften wir durcheinander. Jedermann
hatte sein eigenes Unglück unter dem Sitz,
griffbereit. Eigentlich schade drum.
Es war so praktisch. Das Wasser
floß aus den Wasserhähnen wie nichts.
Wißt ihr noch? Einfach betäubt
von unsern winzigen Gefühlen,
aßen wir wenig. Hätten wir nur geahnt,
daß das alles vorbei sein würde
in fünf Minuten, das Roastbeef Wellington
hätte uns anders, ganz anders geschmeckt.

Short History of the Bourgeoisie

That was the moment when, without
noticing it, for five minutes
we were vastly rich, magnificent
and electric, air-conditioned in July,
or, in case it was November,
the flown-in Finnish wood blazed
in Tudor fireplaces. Funny,
it was all there, just flew in
by itself, as it were. Elegant
we were, no one could bear us.
We threw solo concerts around,
chips, orchids in cellophane. Clouds
that said, I. Unique!

Flights everywhere. Even our sighs
went on credit cards. Like sailors
we bandied curses. Each one
had his own misfortune under the seat,
ready to grab at it. A waste, really.
It was so practical. Water
flowed out of taps just like that.
Remember? Simply stunned
by our tiny emotions,
we ate little. If only we'd guessed
that all this would pass
in five minutes, the roast beef Wellington
would have tasted different, quite different.

Die Frösche von Bikini

Bohrende Fragen, Gestichel, Einwände:
Er halte inne, höre zu, aufmerksam,
lasse sich alles gesagt sein.
Die unerfüllbaren Forderungen
seien berechtigt.
Die Vorwürfe zu entkräften
sei er nicht in der Lage.
Nur eines bitte er höflich
nicht zu erwähnen: seine Probleme.

Wenn er das schon höre—
vorgestern erst, auf dem Heimweg,
zwischen Ambulanzen und Betonmischmaschinen,
durch die halb offene Tür einer Telefonzelle:
»Meine Probleme«—
ein quakendes Geräusch aus der Leitung,
oder auch auf Kongressen,
in therapeutischer Absicht:
»Wege zur Selbsterfahrung«—
offenbar gar kein Vergleich
mit anderen Wirbeltieren!

Nein, auf Selbsterfahrung lege er keinen Wert,
und Probleme habe er nicht,
wenigstens keine »eigenen«. Plötzlich,
am Abend, die Übelkeit ohne Ursache,
oder »die Unterdrückung« (im Allgemeinen),
oder die Kreidestriche im Scheinwerferlicht
um einen Fleck auf der Autobahn—
er meine besonders die Kreidestriche—:
was daran Besonderes sei,
vermöge er nicht zu erkennen.
Er müsse auf seine Stimme hören,
das sei alles.

The Frogs of Bikini

Nagging questions, taunting remarks, objections:
He'd stop short, listen attentively,
take stock, take notice.
The demands made upon him, fully justified,
were impossible to comply with;
to refute the recriminations
was out of the question.
Just one thing he'd rather not have mentioned:
his problems.

That sort of talk was getting too much for him—
only the day before yesterday,
on his way home,
amongst cement mixers and ambulances,
through the half-open door of a phone box:
'My personal problems'—
a croaking sound from the earphone,
or at conventions:
'Our path to self-awareness'
(by way of therapy)—
apparently all these animals
were beyond comparison
with other vertebrates!

No, he couldn't care less
about 'being aware',
and as far as he was concerned,
there were no problems to speak of,
at least not 'personal' ones.
Just the sudden attack of nausea,
unaccountably, at night,
the sense of 'repression' (in general),
or else the chalk-marks seen in the glare
of the head-lights round a dark spot
on the motorway: the chalk-marks
gave him food for thought, but to his mind
there was nothing 'personal' about them.
He'd have to listen to the Voice in his head,
that was all.

Gewisse Geister im Schrank, gewisse Adressen—
da draußen, auf einer staubigen Bank
am Mariannenplatz—
ein Pakistani schlurft vorbei—
Ecke Oranienburger würgt etwas,
privat, unbemerkt, erstickt
und steht nicht mehr auf.

Während ich, sagt er,
weil mir nichts anderes übrigbleibt,
horche, auf jene Stimme,
auf daß sie mir sage wohin,
mit wem, wozu—*meine* Stimme,
sagt er, die sich nicht vernehmen läßt,
und das unterscheidet mich von den Irren—,
weint Fräulein Bausch vor dem Spiegel,
magersüchtig, Ansbacher Straße,
vierter Stock, Gartenhaus—
er deute das alles nur an.

Allzu viele Verluste, süße Isolation,
manches, in dem er nicht mehr enthalten sei;
ferner das Alter, die Wiederholungen
und das Geld. Allerdings, behauptet er,
suchte ich, schuftete, schimpfte,
war ehrgeizig wie ein Idiot,
wurde verlassen, verließ,
und wollte alles zerbrechen.

Damals sei der Hunger größer gewesen.
Zerbrochen habe er nichts.
Ob Wiederholungen so etwas Schlechtes seien,
wisse er nicht genau.
Ohne Zwangsvorstellung
gebe es keine Liebe und keine Arbeit.

Das ist von mir! ruft Engelchen,
das könne von mir sein! das ist gut!—
bekifft, rote Flecken im Gesicht—,
wirft das Buch weg, schminkt sich,
rauft sich die Haare. Dieser Geruch
aus dem Schlafzimmer,

Certain skeletons in cupboards, certain addresses—
out there, on a dusty bench,
Berlin, Mariannenplatz—
a Pakistani shuffling by—
on the corner of Oranienburger Straße
something will choke, privately, unnoticed,
be quietly throttled, not to get up again.

While I, he says, am harkening,
since I cannot help it, to the Voice,
hoping to be told where to go,
with whom, what for—*my* Voice,
he says, which I cannot hear,
and that's where I differ from the insane—,
Fräulein Bausch will weep
in front of the looking-glass,
anorectic, Ansbacher Straße,
fourth floor, rear wing—
he'd rather not enlarge on the subject.

All too many losses, sweet isolation,
things which have ceased to concern him,
not to mention his age, those recurrences
and money. It is true, he goes on,
I have searched and toiled, insulted everybody,
I was keen like an idiot,
I deserted and was deserted,
I had a mind to smash everything.

I used to be hungrier then. In the event
nothing much got smashed.
Whether recurrence was such a bad thing
he'd now be less sure.
As far as he could see, without *idées fixes*
there would be neither work nor love.

That's what I always say! Engelchen cries,
my very words! Exactly!
Stoned, with red spots on his cheeks,
he throws the book away, paints his face,
tears his hair. What is this smell
from the bedroom? Ammonia? Gas?

was ist da? Ammoniak, Gas?
Macht doch die Fenster auf, schnell,
oder schlagt die Tür ein—
merkt denn kein Nachbar was?
Aber die Droysenstraße
liegt völlig verlassen da.

Im August, an entlegenen Stellen,
Schilf und so weiter, Teichlinsen,
höre er, im Licht eines Satelliten,
voller Genugtuung nach Programmschluß
den Fröschen zu. Restbestände.
Diese Vorliebe für alte Häuser,
alte Freiheiten, aussterbende Tiere.
Nichts Besonderes. Aber das Recht
zu quaken und nicht zu quaken—
ihm liege es nun einmal am Herzen,
er bestehe darauf.

Am hellen Nachmittag, anderswo,
verdunkelte Räume. Hier
sind die Vorhänge dick, die Nadeln
glänzen, die Wandtafel mit den Linien
rollt sich im Rauch, es riecht
nach Kampfer. Tiefe Stiche
unter die Haut, natürlich
zum Wohle des Ganzen.
Unblutig lächelt der Akupunkteur.

Oder jene Sitzungen,
auf denen es üblich war,
im Namen der Arbeiterklasse
einander das Nasenbein einzuschlagen,
im übertragenen Sinne natürlich—

Und nun, mein Lieber, haben Sie resigniert?
Nach längerem Nachdenken antwortet er:
Ich bin immer noch da. Und:
Es ist an mir, wie ich glaube,
eine gewisse Beharrlichkeit festzustellen.

Quick! Open the windows
or break down the door—where are the neighbours?
Don't they realise what's going on?
Not a soul in sight.
Droysenstraße lies deserted.

Then again, in August, and in remote places,
full of bulrushes, duckweed, etcetera,
he'd listen, after all stations have closed down,
to his heart's content, in the gleam of a satellite,
to the frogs. Residues.
His predilection for old houses,
old liberties, animals on the brink of extinction.
Nothing personal. Just the right
to croak or not to croak—
he'd insist on it.

Somewhere else again, in the afternoon,
a shuttered room. The thick curtains,
the glittering needles, the wall chart
with the twisted lines basking
in the smoke, the camphor fumes.
Deep forays beneath the skin,
all, of course, to the ultimate good
of the patient, and at the last twist
the acupuncturist's bloodless smile.

Or he'd remember the caucus sessions
where it was customary
to bash in each other's nasal bones
in the name of the working class—
figuratively speaking, of course.

And now, my dear chap? Have you given in?
After careful reflection he'd answer:
I'm still around. Observing me closely,
you'll find me pig-headed, I believe.

Sich Abfinden sei etwas für Optimisten
oder für Tote, etwas Jenseitiges,
komme mithin im Kosmos nicht vor,
sei auch in Friedenau,
dem Stadtviertel, wo er wohne,
eine unbekannte Erscheinung—
ganz im Gegensatz zu Amokläufen,
Tablettenvergiftungen, Psychosen,
kurz, Tathandlungen, Ausbrüchen,
Zerfleischung und Gegenwehr.

Nichts bleibt, wie es ist,
glücklicherweise.
Nicht nur der Frosch,
auch die Froschforschung
kann schließlich zurückblicken
auf Errungenschaften.
Ein ohrenbetäubendes Spektakel.

Auch er werde immer besser,
unwillkürlich, genau wie die Krankheiten,
wie die Zahnkrem, das soziale Netz.
»Auf erweiterter Stufenleiter,«
höre er seine Freunde rufen
von nebenan—»naturwüchsig«—,
und er rufe zurück: Eureka!
Meine Guten, nennt mir doch etwas,
das nicht naturwüchsig wäre.

Vom Laich zur Kaulquappe,
von der Kaulquappe zum Frosch,
vom Frosch zum Fossil.
Ach, was wären wir ohne die erste Evolution,
und die zweite, was wäre sie ohne uns!
Ohne quak wäre quak nicht quak,
und umgekehrt. Wohin er auch höre,
keine Stimme, nur
der wunderbare Gesang der Mutanten.

According to his lights, to give in
is a course fit for optimists
and for the dead, something transcendent
in short, not to be found in our universe,
let alone in Friedenau, his own
quarter of Berlin—where on the other hand
all sorts of rash acts abound,
family murders, psychoses,
sleeping pill suicides, i.e. mayhem,
havoc and self-defence.

Nothing, fortunately,
remains as it is.
Not only the frogs can look back
on splendid achievements.
Frog ethology, too,
has made great strides.
Altogether a deafening show.

He himself, would advance, as well,
involuntarily, just like the diseases
around him, like toothpaste
and social security, on a higher scale.
'Naturally,' his friends would shout
from next door, and he'd call back:
'Eureka! My dear fellows, can you think
of anything outside of Nature?

From spawn to tadpole,
from tadpole to frog,
from frog to fossil.
Where would we be without the first,
and where would the second evolution
end up without us? Croak
would hardly be croak without croak,
and vice versa. Whichever way
he'd cock his ear, no voice to be heard,
save the wondrous song of the mutants.

Ohrenbetäubend und immer neu
ineinander verbissen
diese subtilen Nahrungsketten,
und weich und stumm
ineinander verschlungen
die grauen Lappen der Rinde.

»Über einige strukturelle Eigentümlichkeiten
des sozialen Verhaltens bei *rana rana*«:
All die Fossilien im Sediment
unseres Gehirns rühren sich,
zappeln, elektrisieren uns:
die Erste, die Zweite, die Dritte Natur,
etc. (N_1, N_2, N_3, ... N_n).

Selbst jene Wolke dort, die er,
vor sich hinmurmelnd, betrachte,
voller Genugtuung, habe sich,
während er murmle, verändert,
naturwüchsig, wattig, fern,
wie gewisse Wörter,
im Aussterben begriffen,
die ihm teuer seien, wie »Wollust«,
»Verlangen«, »Begierde«,—Zustände,
instabil wie das Positron,
doch längst nicht so gut erforscht.

Auch jenes wachsverklebte Bett,
jenes Zimmer, schwarz gestreift
vom Ruß der Kerzen, hat eine Adresse;
ihr blakendes Licht,
die achtlos wechselnden Tageszeiten—
ich werde das Haus nicht wiederfinden.

Oder Bikini. Er denke oft an Bikini.
Alles sei wieder da,
dreißig Jahre nach der Apokalypse,
»auf erweiterter Stufenleiter«.
Laubfrösche, taufrisch,
unaufhaltsam. Ein Klettern sei das,
eine Akrobatik, sogar das Wetter
mache Fortschritte. Das Weiß
der Strände, menschenleer—

Deafening and forever novel
the subtle food-chains
locking their teeth,
and soft and silently twisting
the grey folds of the cortex.

'On some structural peculiarities
in the social behaviour of *rana rana*':
All those fossils in the sediment of our brain
begin to quiver, to quake, to electrify us:
First Nature, Second Nature, Third,
etcetera (N_1, N_2, N_3,...N_n).

Even the cloud over there,
which he'd contemplate to his heart's content,
talking softly to himself, would change,
'naturally', fuzzily, in the distance
just like certain words, on the brink
of extinction, words dear to him,
like 'Longing', 'Desire', 'Lust',
standing for states as short-lived
as the position, though
far less well-studied by science.

The bed that used to be plastered
with wax droppings, the room darkly striped
by the soot of candles, must have an address
somewhere, their fluttering light,
the times of the day passing unnoticed—
I shall not find the door again.

Or else Bikini. He'd find himself often
thinking of it. Things in Bikini
were back to normal, everything had returned,
thirty years after the apocalypse,
'on a higher scale'. Tree frogs,
fresh as daisies, scrambling up the scale
to the top, progressively,
like acrobats. There's no stopping them.
Even the weather will improve in time.
The beaches white, untouched by human feet.

Wie am gestirnten Himmel über uns
die harte Strahlung, der Helium-Flash,
die hemmungslose Verschwendung,
so auch hienieden. Das Glück—
er wage es kaum, das Wort
in den Mund zu nehmen—, das Glück,
selten, plötzlich, unzweifelhaft
(je nach Chromosomensatz, Klassenlage,
Hormonspiegel, Uhrzeit),
sei vielleicht das letzte Verbrechen.

Der Mann, der am Sonntag verzweifeln muß,
weil am Sonntag das Telefonieren billiger ist,
der Mann, der an den Worten seiner Frau,
einer Fremden hängt, wie an einem Strick,
dieser Mann sei er. Du
hättest nicht zu betteln, ich
hätte dich nicht zu schlagen, wir
hätten einander nicht zu verlieren brauchen—
das alles am Telefon, das alles am Sonntag,
und anderen Leuten, das wisse er wohl,
schiene dieser Abgrund vielleicht
nur ein paar Zentimeter tief—

Gleich bin ich fertig; an meinem Leumund
liegt mir nichts; mein Abschreiber,
mein Polyp, mein Blutegel, Professor Fels,
der »über mich arbeitet«—einer von denen—,
siehe, er langweilt sich schon.
Im übrigen bin ich Zuschauer. Ja,
ich schaue zu. Diese Pflichtübungen,
Maiandachten und Prozessionen,
behauptet er, habe er satt. Bis zum Hals
in löchrigen Schnürstiefeln
eine Halde von alten Schuhen zu überqueren
mit durchgelaufenen Sohlen—
wenn das der Neue Mensch sei,
dann lieber nicht.

Der hat leicht reden.
Und wie stehts mit dem Geld?

Dissipation, extravagance, just like above us
the starry skies, full of hard radiation,
of helium-flashes, life here below
goes on lavishly. Bliss—
he'd hardly dare utter the word—,
bliss, rare, sudden, indubitable
(determined, naturally, by chromosome sets,
class, hormone levels, and the time of the day)
may be the ultimate crime.

The man who's got to shelve his despair
until Sunday, because it is cheaper
to call long distance on Sundays,
the man who hangs on the lips of his woman,
a stranger's lips, as on a rope,
that's me, he shouts. For no earthly reason
you begged me, I beat you, we lost each other—
all this on the telephone, on a Sunday—
and as he was well aware, this abyss
would have seemed, to the rest of the world,
rather shallow—

Don't worry, I shall be done presently,
I do not care about my good name;
my scribe, my parasite, my leech,
Professor Fels, who is 'working on me',
look, he must be bored by now with his thesis,
Anyway, I'm just an onlooker,
standing by, peering. All those marches,
devotions and exercises he claims to be sick of.
If you have to cross a heap of old shoes,
on wornout soles, up to the neck
in battered lace-boots
in order to become a New Man—
why, he'd rather not.

Oh well, it is easy for you to talk!
What about your bank account?

Wohnungen, Wagen, Steuerbescheide:
ja, meine Liebste, es stimmt,
ich habe manchmal daran gedacht,
an die Sicherheit, daß ich nicht lache,
wie der Laubfrosch im Glas.
Aber sie beruhigt mich nicht,
die Sicherheit, sie macht Angst.
Daher, glaub mir, kommt meine Ruhe nicht.
Sie nickt verächtlich und geht,
die eine, die mit den hellen Augen,
aber die andere, die keine Furcht hat
und klüger ist, sie wird mir glauben.
Und es ist wahr, daß ich niemanden finde,
der zu beneiden wäre.

Wahr ist (*stockend; niedergeschlagen*),
daß ich den Schmerz nicht verstehen kann
in eurem Namen. Teilnahmslos
bin ich nicht, sondern geständig.
(*Matt. Zu sich selber.*) Merkwürdig,
was einem alles sympathisch wird mit der Zeit.
Was alles von selber verschwindet.
Was einen dauert. (*Pause. Drohend.*)
Aber ich kann auch anders.
Laßt mir Herrn Dr. Benn in Ruhe!
Belle-Alliance-Straße, alle Kassen.
Seine Patienten jedenfalls
haben sich nie über ihn beklagt.

(*Leise.*) Bis zu einem gewissen Grad
mach ich gemeinsame Sache mit euch.
Aber wir wollen nicht übertreiben.
(*Sehr bestimmt.*) Meine Ruhe,
soweit davon die Rede sein kann,
ist nicht terroristisch. (*Brüsk.*)
Was, Lichtblicke? Oh,
Lichtblicke gibt es genug. Nur da nicht,
wo ihr sie sucht, oder ich.
Utopien? Gewiß, aber wo?
Wir sehen sie nicht. Wir fühlen sie nur
wie das Messer im Rücken.

It is perfectly true, my dear girl,
I too, at times, have been thinking
of cars, houses, tax returns,
of putting an end to my worries,
of security, like a frog in his jar.
What a joke! But in the event,
it gave me no peace, security,
it worried me stiff. No, my calm,
believe me, is of another kind.
She will give me a nod of scorn
and turn away, the bright-eyed girl,
but the other one who is fearless
and wise, she will believe me.
And it is true that I never found
any man I could envy.

It is true (*slight stammer, dejected look*)
that I cannot understand pain
on your behalf. It is not
as if I did not care. I plead guilty.
(*Tired voice. To himself.*) Extraordinary,
the things one comes to sympathise with
in the long run. The things that vanish.
The things one regrets. (*Pause. Menacing tone.*)
But I am not a sucker! And I ask you
to leave Dr Benn alone.
He treated no private patients,
and no one who came to him
ever complained.

(*Softly.*) Up to a point I cast in my lot
with yours. Solidarity by all means.
But let's not exaggerate.
(*Pointedly.*) My calm, as far as it goes,
is not based on terror. (*Brusquely.*)
What? Silver linings? Oh,
there's plenty of them. Not,
of course, where you or I
would look for them. Utopias?
Certainly. But where are they?
Out of sight. We can only feel them
like a knife sticking in our back.

Unter diesen Umständen müsse er sich
zuweilen der Stimme enthalten.
Er höre die Stecknadeln fallen,
während die Frösche sich heiser schrien
in den Bombenkratern des Fortschritts,
wo der Regen neue Tümpel bildet,
naturwüchsig: N_n sive deus.
Nicht ohne Zuversicht erwarte er
die Abschaffung unsrer Abschaffungen.
Ein schöner Septembertag.
Klammer zu. Ende der Abschweifung.

Seine Lieblingsdroge
sei die Aufmerksamkeit.
Auf die tägliche Prise
von ideologischem Kokain
könne er notfalls verzichten;
und wenn es schon nicht abgehe ohne Moral—
die seine bestehe darin,
nicht zu ermüden. Aufmerksam
wie seine Freundin beim Schminken,
wie der Moskito im Schlafzimmer,
wie der Spitzel vor jedermanns Haus,
wie der Frosch, der ins Wasser springt
bei der geringsten Bewegung,
(und aus ähnlichen Gründen)
betrachte er alles, was der Fall sei.
Seine fünfundzwanzig Sinne reichten hin,
ein Gehirn zu beschäftigen.

Nebenan Kirchenlieder,
gesungen von ältlichen Adventisten.
Friedenau. Wolkenfelder.
Die Massaker, zu denen »es kommt«.
»Historisch«. Sag mir doch etwas,
das nicht »historisch« wäre.
Er murmelt das alles vor sich hin, zerstreut,
abgelenkt von den hundertzwölftausend Farben,
die sein Auge unterscheiden kann.

Under these circumstances
every now and then he'd have to abstain.
He could hear a pin falling
while the frogs shout themselves hoarse
in the bomb craters of progress,
where the rain will form ever new ponds,
naturally: N_n *sive deus*.
He'd look forward, hopefully,
to the aboliton of our abolitions.
A marvellous day in September.
Parenthesis closed. End of digression.

His favourite drug, he maintains,
is alertness, the daily dose
of ideological cocaine
he'd just as well do without;
and if some sort of morals are indispensable,
as they say, well, his own would forbid him
to flag. Attentively,
like his girlfriend painting her lips,
like the mosquito hovering in the bedroom,
like the plain-clothes man at the front door,
like the frog who will jump into the pond
at the slightest sign of trouble
(and for similar reasons)
he'd have an eye on everything that transpires.
His twenty-five senses were quite sufficient
to keep his brain busy.

Hymns from next door,
sung by elderly adventists.
Herds of clouds passing by
over Berlin-Friedenau.
The massacres which 'result',
'historically'. Tell me something
that would be outside of History.
He's absent-minded, he mumbles distracted
by the hundred and twelve thousand shades of colour
which his eye can discern.

Einmal, Richtung Bodensee, an der Ausfahrt,
war etwas Weiches zu sehen,
glitzernd im Scheinwerferlicht.
Rettungsfahrzeuge, Männer mit Stangen,
mit Netzen. Ein schwaches Geräusch
unter den Rädern, schlürfend, feucht,
übertönt im Fond von der Kadenz,
Mozart, Klavierkonzert, zweiter Satz—
diese ländliche Gegend,
Flach- und Zwischenmoor,
für die Frösche auf ihrer Wanderung
war sie Bikini.

Da ich aber beschlossen habe,
unauffällig zu sein,
bescheiden, maßvoll und höflich,
und da es nicht üblich ist,
einander laut zu verfluchen,
werde ich meinen Zettel
nicht auseinanderfalten,
die Liste der Ungeheuer
in winziger Schrift, wie das Vaterunser,
in einen Kirschkern geritzt,—
auch weil der Zettel, entfaltet,
uns alle bedecken würde.

Verschwendete Flüche tragen nicht weit.
Ich spare, ich kratze zusammen
das, was ich habe, ich laure,
bis er die Glastür aufstößt
mit seinem glänzenden weißen Gesicht,
der Pharisäer, der ewiglich
bessere Mensch, die Sau
mit dem guten Gewissen:
ihm werfe ich meinem Fluch
vor den Bauch, meine Bombe.

Wer ist hier der Pharisäer?
Wie alt sind Sie überhaupt?
Meinen Sie etwa mich?
Sind Sie verrückt,
einfach hier anzurufen
am Sonntagnachmittag?

Once, on the way to Lake Constance,
on the motorway exit, something soft
was to be seen, shining
in the glare of the head-lights.
Emergency patrols, men
brandishing poles and nets.
There was a soft swish underneath the wheels,
something moist, drowned
by the notes of the cadence, Mozart,
piano concerto, second movement—
this part of the country,
marshlands, moors,
for the frogs on their last migration
it was Bikini.

Since I have decided, once and for all,
to be inconspicuous,
modest, well-tempered and civil,
and since it is not good form
to curse one another shrilly,
I shall not unfold at present
my piece of paper, my list
of monsters, drawn up in minute script
like the Lord's Prayer engraved
onto a cherry-stone—
if only because my piece of paper,
unfolded, would cover us all.

Spent curses will not carry far.
I save them, I scrape together
all I have, I lurk,
until he pushes the glass-door open,
he with the shiny white face,
the Pharisee, the eternal do-gooder,
the self-righteous pig.
Then I will thrust my curse,
my bomb, in his lap.

What do you mean by Pharisee?
Are you of age? Why
are you looking at me?
Are you mad, to ring me up,
a perfect stranger,
on a Sunday afternoon?

Was soll das heißen, Ungeheuer?
Von jetzt an nehme ich jedes Wort,
das Sie sagen, auf Band.

Das alles ist schon eine Weile her.
Hier, weit draußen, Altbau,
Blick auf den Garten,
sind keine Frösche zu hören.
Ich schaue zu. Ich merke, was los ist.
Diese Wolke dort drüben stirbt
vollkommen still. Ich habe verlernt
zu sagen: »Im Gegenteil«.
Hier ist nichts los. Ich warte,
ruhig. Irgendwo kämpfen die Feinde,
nach wie vor, die alten Feinde,
immer ähnlicher einer dem andern,
gleichgültiger, ferner,
immer woanders.

Aber ich bin doch hier,
ich hänge an euch, ich brüte doch
über euerm Brüten. Im toten Winkel,
hinter den ringsum aufgetürmten,
undurchschaubaren, sperrigen Möbeln
atmet es, eingepreßt—
verstellt euch nicht! Ihr hört es
so gut wie ich: ein, aus,
ein, aus – dieser Blasebalg,
den wir nicht sehen können—,
ich kann ihn nicht sehen,
wie er da liegt im Staub und regelmäßig,
regelmäßig, regelmäßig ächzt, ledern
keucht—, davon, davon
erzähle ich euch, dumpf und regelmäßig.

Ich will nicht, daß ihr ihn tauft,
bezeichnet, diskutiert, diesen Balg.
Horcht lieber, mir zuliebe,
ich bitte euch, oder lacht.

Looking for monsters, here
of all places! From now on
all you say will be taped!

In the mean time, out here,
where the houses are old and worn,
and the back-gardens overgrown,
no frogs are in evidence.
I am looking on, I have an eye
on everything that goes on.
The cloud over there dies
in perfect stillness. I've given up
saying: 'On the contrary'.
Nothing much is going on.
I wait, calmly. Somewhere else
there are enemies fighting,
the old enemies, resembling each other
more and more in the process,
more and more indifferent and remote,
somewhere else.

But I am still here, I hold forth,
I cling to you, I brood
over your broodings. In the dead angle
behind the unwieldy, impenetrable
furniture towering all around me
I can hear something breathing,
a wheeze—don't pretend
that you cannot hear it:
in, out, in, out, a pair of bellows
out of sight. I cannot see it.
It's crouching there in the dust
and evenly, evenly, evenly groaning,
leathery, gasping,
that's it, that's what I'm telling you
dully and even.

I do not want you to name it,
to label it, to discuss it,
this pair of bellows over there
in the corner. Just listen,
for my sake, for your sake,
I beseech you, listen to it or laugh.

Lacht nur! Das macht doch nichts.
Zeit vergeht. Wenn ihr wollt,
halten wir einander den Mund zu,
wenn euch das lieber ist, auch die Ohren—

oder ihr schnupft, kaut, raucht, spritzt,
ich mache mit, ich bin dabei,
wir haben Zeit, macht das Licht an,
wer baden will, badet,
ich sage nicht: »Im Gegenteil«,
im Gegenteil! Werft die Kleider weg,
saugt aneinander
wer nicht will, hat schon,
feuchtet euch an,
jeder nach seinen Bedürfnissen,
fünf Minuten vor zwölf.

Das könne lange dauern.
Er sei kein Prophet,
über manches rede er nicht,
er deute nur an, warte, und seine Stimme
lasse er nur deshalb erschallen,
weil sonst keine Stimme zu hören sei,
keine Angst, keine Tränen,
er sei ja da, er bleibe.

Ich bleibe, sagt er,
wir sagen einander ins Ohr,
was wir gewollt hätten,
wenn wir nicht dem Warten verfallen wären,
dem atemlosen selbstsüchtigen Horchen
auf unsern Atemzug, wie er dort hinten
rassle, im toten Winkel, innen
rassle, regelmäßig
rassle.

Laugh if you like. It does not matter.
Time passes. If you will,
we might gag each other,
or, if you prefer, plug our ears.

Or you could snuff, chew, smoke, shoot,
I am with you, I do as you do
there is plenty of time,
put on the lights, if you will,
he who wants a bath, let him take it,
I don't say: 'On the contrary',
on the contrary! Throw off your clothes,
suck one another,
take it or leave it, cream,
to everyone according to his needs,
it is five to twelve.

This sort of thing might go on
for quite some time.
He'd not qualify as a prophet.
There were things he'd rather not talk about.
He'd just drop a hint every now and then,
he'd wait, and his voice would resound
only because there was no other voice
to be heard, no panic, no tears.
He was here to stay.

I am here to stay, he says,
let's whisper in one another's ear
what we might have wanted to do
if we'd not succumbed to the waiting,
to our breathless, selfish harkening
to our very own breath,
to the rattle over there
rattling evenly,
in the dead angle,
the rattle within.

Automat

Er zieht Zigaretten
für ein paar Mark Zigaretten

Er zieht den Krebs
er zieht die Apartheid
er zieht ein paar entfernte Massaker

Er zieht und zieht
doch indem er zieht
verschwindet alles was er zieht

Auch die Zigaretten verschwinden

Er blickt den Automaten an
Er sieht sich selber
Für einen Augenblick
sieht er aus wie ein Mensch

Dann verschwindet er wieder
Mit einem Klacks
fallen die Zigaretten

Er ist verschwunden
Es war nur ein Augenblick
Es war eine Art von Glück

Er ist verschwunden
Unter dem was er gezogen hat
liegt er begraben

Vending Machine

He puts four dimes into the slot
he gets himself some cigarettes

He gets cancer
he gets apartheid
he gets a couple of far-away massacres

He gets more and more
for his four dimes
but for a moment all the things disappear

Even the cigarettes

He looks at the vending machine
He sees himself
For a fleeting moment
he almost looks like a man

Then very soon he is gone again
with a little click
there are his cigarettes

He has disappeared
it was just a fleeting moment
some kind of sudden bliss

He has disappeared
he is gone
buried under all the stuff he got
for his four dimes

Die Glasglocke

Besonders morgens ist, in den Gewächshäusern,
schräg gegenüber, wo Gurken gedeihen,
ohne Rücksicht auf Mord und Totschlag,
ich gähne freudig, alles in Ordnung.
Aus meinem Hahn, dessen kaltes Email
KALT sagt, schwarz auf weiß, fließt wie immer
das Wasser warm. Der Trödler schräg gegenüber
zieht seinen Rolladen hoch, donnernd.
Ich sehe Leute, die kehren, backen,
nageln, zählen, waschen und schreiben.
Ich schreibe, ordentlich. Möbelpacker
sind da, rollschuhfahrende Kinder. Warum
so ordentlich? so gewaltlos? als wäre
nichts der Fall? Am offenen Fenster
stimmt jemand ein Klavier, ich kann nur
seine Hände sehen, wie nackt sie sind
und wie weich! Ein Kühlschrank beginnt
zu summen, Züge sind pünklich, es dreht sich
unter der glasigen Haube des Zählers
lautlos ein Ring, in der Morgensonne
glitzernd. Ein Mann steht, winzig
und hellblau, schräg gegenüber, hoch
auf dem Dach, er wippt, er bückt sich,
er klopft an das verzinkte Blech, ich sehe
ihn klopfen, aber ich höre nichts.
Ein scheckiger Frieden dehnt sich, weich
und winzig, am Vormittag, halb betäubt
von der Sonne, in einer alltäglichen Trance,
und streckt sich gelb, wie die Katze
auf dem Zementsack, schräg gegenüber.

The Bell Jar

In the mornings especially, in the greenhouses
across the road, where cucumbers thrive,
regardless of assault and murder,
I yawn happily, everything is normal.
From my tap, whose cold enamel
says COLD, in bold letters, as usual the water
runs warm. The junk merchant across the road
with a thundering noise, raises his shutter.
I see people who sweep, bake,
nail, count, wash and write.
I write, normally. Furniture removers
are here, roller-skating children. Why
so normal? So unviolent? as though
nothing were wrong? At the open window
someone tunes a piano. I can see
only his hands, how naked they are,
and how soft! A refrigerator begins
to hum, trains are on time, under
the meter's glass cover a disk
revolves without a sound and glitters
in the morning sunshine. A man, tiny
and pale blue, across the road,
stands high up on the roof, he teeters, he bends down,
he taps the galvanised sheeting, I see
him tap, but I hear nothing.
A mottled quiet spreads out, tiny
and soft, into the morning, half dazed
by the sun, in an every-day trance,
and yellowly stretches, like the cat
on that bag of cement, across the road.

Nicht Zutreffendes streichen

Was deine Stimme so flach macht
so dünn und so blechern
das ist die Angst
etwas Falsches zu sagen

oder immer dasselbe
oder das zu sagen was alle sagen
oder etwas Unwichtiges
oder Wehrloses
oder etwas das mißverstanden werden könnte
oder den falschen Leuten gefiele
oder etwas Reaktionäres
oder etwas Kitschiges
oder etwas Dummes
oder etwas schon Dagewesenes
etwas Altes

Hast du es denn nicht satt
aus lauter Angst
aus lauter Angst vor der Angst
etwas Falsches zu sagen

immer das Falsche zu sagen?

Delete the Inapplicable

What makes your voice so flat
so thin and tinny
is your fear
of saying the wrong thing

or always the same thing
or saying what everyone says
or saying something unimportant
or something vulnerable
or something that could be misunderstood
or that could please the wrong people
or something reactionary
or something in bad taste
or something stupid
or something old hat
something stale

Aren't you tired of it—
only for fear
only for fear of the fear
of saying the wrong thing

saying the wrong thing always?

Der Kamm

Sie blenden mich. Sie sind schön im Vorübergehn.
Ich bewundere Sie, im Schnee, an der Haltestelle,
wie Sie sich morgens geschmückt haben, militant
und mit letzter Kraft. Eine, die nicht hinkt,
die sich nicht bücken will nach dem Groschen
im Schnee, die ihre Gebrechen verbirgt, unheilbar,
wie ich. Und diesen Kamm, der in Ihrem Haar glänzt.
Flammendes Schildpatt. Allerdings, dem
fehlen auch ein paar Zähne.—Ach bewundern,
das kann ein jeder sagen.—Verzeihen Sie,
ich meine nur das, was niemand braucht,
was keinerlei Eindruck an Ihnen macht:
den Zehennagel, der langsam gedeiht, das Haar,
die feuchte, hinfällige Haut; kleine Ströme,
nervöse Absonderungen, vorübergehend
wie Ihre Seele, die nicht geschickt ist,
mürbe, von Tabletten zerfressen, erbsenklein,
verloren in Ihrem Brustkorb. Ja, natürlich,
wir müssen fort, haben keine Zeit. Ich weiß.
Was wollte ich sagen? Ja. Weinen Sie weiter.
Ihr Kamm!—Wie bitte?—Sie haben ihn
fallenlassen. Dort auf dem Pflaster liegt er,
wo vorhin der Schnee war, geheimnisvoll
und gewöhnlich. Bald wird er zertreten sein.
Das ist unvermeidlich. Das kann ein jeder sagen.
Ich mache keinerlei Eindruck. Ich sehe ihn
in der Sonne glänzen. Hören Sie nicht auf mich.
Meine Wörter bücken sich nicht. Sie sind
nicht dazu da, etwas aufzuheben. Sie sind da,
eine Weile lang. Es kann sie ein jeder sagen.

The Comb

You dazzle me. You are beautiful in passing.
I admire you, in snow, at the bus stop,
how you've adorned yourself in the morning, militant
and with a last effort. One who does not limp,
who refuses to stoop for the penny
dropped into snow, who conceals her ailments, incurable
as I am. And this comb that shines in your hair.
Blazing tortoiseshell. True enough, it too
lacks a few teeth. Oh, admire—
anyone can say that.—Forgive me,
I mean only that which nobody needs,
that about you which makes no impression at all:
the toenail that slowly thrives, the hair,
the moist, perishable skin; little currents,
nervous secretions, ephemeral
as your soul that's devoid of skill,
brittle, riddled with pills, tiny as a pea,
lost in your ribcage. Yes, of course,
we must move on, have no time. I know.
What did I want to say? Yes. Don't stop crying.
Your comb!—Pardon?—You've
dropped it. There it lies, on the pavement,
where the snow was a moment ago, mysterious
and commonplace. Soon it will snap, trodden on.
That can't be helped. Anyone can say that.
I make no impression at all. I see it
gleam in the sun. Don't listen to me.
My words don't bend down. They're not here
for picking up things. They are here,
for a while. Anyone can say them.

Die Kleider

Da liegen sie, still und katzenhaft
in der Sonne, nachmittags,
deine Kleider, ausgebeult,
traumlos, wie ein Zufall.
Sie riechen nach dir, schwach,
sehen dir beinah ähnlich.
Deinen Schmutz überliefern sie,
deine schlechten Gewohnheiten,
die Spur deiner Ellenbogen.
Sie haben Zeit, atmen nicht,
sind übrig, schlaff, voller Knöpfe,
Eigenschaften und Flecken.
In der Hand eines Polizisten,
einer Schneiderin, eines Archäologen
gäben sie ihre Nähte preis,
ihre nichtigen Geheimnisse.
Aber wo du bist, ob du leidest,
was du mir immer hast sagen wollen
und nie gesagt hast,
ob du wiederkommst, ob das,
was geschah, aus Liebe geschah
oder aus Not oder Vergeßlichkeit,
und warum dies alles so,
wie es gekommen ist,
gekommen ist,
als es ums nackte Leben ging,
ob du tot bist, oder ob
du dir nur die Haare wäschst,
das sagen sie nicht.

Clothes

Here they lie, still and cat-like
in the sun, in the afternoon,
your clothes, baggy,
undreaming, as if by chance.
They smell of you, faintly,
they almost take after you,
give away your dirt,
your bad habits,
the trace of your elbows.
They take their time, don't breathe,
are left over, limp, full of buttons,
properties, stains.
In the hands of a policeman,
a dressmaker, an archaeologist
they would reveal their seams,
their idle secrets. But where you are,
whether you suffer, what
you had always wanted to tell me
and never did, whether
what happened has happened
for love's sake or from need
or from negligence, and why
all this has come about as it did
when it was a question
of saving our skin,
whether you are dead by now
or have gone to wash your hair,
they do not tell.

Besuch bei Ingres

Heute hätte er für das ZK gemalt, oder für die Paramount,
je nachdem. Aber damals schwitzten die Gangster noch
unter dem Hermelin, und die Hochstapler ließen sich krönen.
Also her mit Insignien, Perlen und Pfauenfedern.

Wir treffen den Künstler sinnend an. Er hat sich ausgestopft
mit »gewählten Gedanken und edlen Leidenschaften«.
Eine mühsame Sache. Teure Sesselchen, Erstes Empire oder Zweites,
je nachdem. Weiches Kinn, weiche Hände, »Griechentum in der
          Seele«.

Sechzig Jahre lang diese kalte Gier, jeder Zoll ein Könner,
bis es erreicht war: die Rosette im Knopfloch, der Ruhm.

Diese Frauen, die sich vor ihm auf dem Marmor winden
wie Robben aus Hefeteig: zwischen Daumen und Zeigefinger
die Brüste gemessen, die Oberfläche studiert wie Plüsch,
Tüll, Spiegeltaft, die Feuchtigkeit in den Augenwinkeln
zwölfmal lasiert wie Gelatine, das Inkarnat glatt
und narkotisch, besser als Kodak: ausgestellt
in der École des Beaux-Arts, eine käufliche Ewigkeit.

Wozu das Ganze? Wozu das Blech der Orde
der fanatische Fleiß, die vergoldeten Adler aus Gips?

Merkwürdig schwammig sieht er mit achtzig aus,
erschöpft, den Zylinderhut in der linken Hand.
»Es war alles umsonst.« Aber aber, verehrter Meister!
Was soll denn der Rahmenmacher, der Glaser von Ihnen denken,
die treue Köchin, der Leichenwäscher? Einzige Antwort:

Er seufzt. Hoch über den Wolken, onirisch, die Finger der Thetis,
die sich wie Würmer ringeln auf Jupiters schwarzem Bart.
Widerwillig werfen wir einen letzten Blick
auf den Künstler—wie kurz seine Beine sind!—
und verlassen auf Zehenspitzen das Atelier.

Visiting Ingres

Today he'd be painting for the Central Committee, or Paramount,
it all depends. But at that time a gangster still sweated
under his ermine, and the con-men had themselves crowned.
So let's have them, the insignia, pearls, the peacock feathers.

We find the artist pensive. He has stuffed himself
with 'choice ideas and noble passions'.
A laborious business. Expensive small armchairs, First or Second
        Empire,
it all depends. Soft chin, soft hands, 'Hellas in his soul'.

For sixty years this cold greed, every inch a craftsman,
till he's achieved it: fame, the rosette in his buttonhole.

These women, writhing in front of him on the marble
like seals made of risen dough: between thumb and forefinger
the breasts measured, the surface studied like plush,
tulle, glossy taffeta, the moisture in the corner of their eyes
glazed twelve times over like gelatine, the flesh colour smooth
and narcotic, better than Kodak: exhibited
in the Ecole des Beaux-Arts, a venal eternity.

What's it all for? What for the tin of his decorations,
the fanatical industry, the gilt plaster eagles?

Curiously bloated he looks at eighty,
worn out, with that top hat in his left hand.
'It was all for nothing'. How can you say that, most honoured Maître!
What will the frame-maker think of you, the glazier?
your faithful cook, the undertaker? His only answer:

A sigh. Far above the clouds, oniric, the fingers of Thetis
that squirm like worms on Jupiter's black beard.
Reluctantly we take a last brief look
at the artist—how short his legs are!—
and tiptoe out of the studio.

Ein Traum

Ich bin auf der Flucht. Ich habe meine Schuhe verloren.
Kirschbäume blühen hinter einem verlassenen Haus.
Der Zaun ist zerbrochen. Meine Füße sind staubig, wund.
Ich sitze im Gras, schlafe ein. Durch das offene Fenster
blicke ich in ein Zimmer, das weiß und kühl ist. Im Traum
sehe ich einen alten Mann barfuß vor einer Leinwand stehen.
Er kehrt mir den Rücken zu. Leicht gebückt
tanzelt er in der Morgensonne und setzt
mit winzigen Strichen rasch ein paar Schuhe hin,
zwinkernd. Wie leicht das geht! Der Geruch
der Farbe ist stechend und fett, und im schrägen Licht
funkelt der nasse Pinsel, jedes einzelne Haar.
Die Zeit vergeht. Weich und rehbraun malt er
die beiden Stiefelchen nebeneinander, etwas versetzt,
in das weiche Gras. Ich rieche das Leder. Die Schlaufen,
die Zungen glänzen matt, ich kann die Haken zählen,
die eisernen Ösen. Außer im Kopf des Malers
und auf seinem Bild sind keine Schuhe da.
Von der Straße her höre ich Leute murmeln,
Hundegebell, Lärm. War das nicht ein Schuß?
Warum tust du das, rufe ich im Traum, was du tust?
Hast du kein Leder?—Er rührt sich nicht.—Ja.
sie sind schön, aber was heißt schön? Bekommst du
Geld dafür?—Ich glaube, er lacht.—Außerdem
sind sie alt und abgetragen.—Er stellt sich taub,
wirft einen Blick auf das Bild, zuckt die Achseln
und geht. Die Stiefelchen stehen warm,
wie zwei schlafende Hasen, im Gras.

A Dream

I am on the run. I have lost my shoes.
Cherry trees in bloom behind a deserted house.
Broken fences. My feet are dusty and sore.
I rest in the grass and go to sleep. Through the open window
I peer into a whitewashed, cool room. In my dream
I see an old man standing barefoot in front of a canvas.
He is turning his back on me. Slightly stooping
he prances in the morning sun and deftly does
with tiny dashes a pair of shoes, blinking.
The ease of it! And the smell of paint!
pungent, oily, the wet brush glittering
in a slanting shaft of light, every single hair.
Time passes. Two little lace-up boots he paints,
soft and reddish brown, side by side, a bit staggered,
onto the soft grass. I smell their leather. I see
the dull sheen of the tongues. I can count
the hooks and the iron eyes. Except in the painter's mind
and on his canvas no shoes are in evidence.
I hear people murmuring on the road outside,
dogs barking, noise. Was there a shot?
Why do you do what you do? I ask in my dream.
Have you no leather?—He does not move.—Beautiful,
yes, they are beautiful, but what does that mean?
Does it pay?—He is laughing now, I believe.—Besides,
they are old and worn.—He ignores what I say,
he glances at the picture, he shrugs
and goes away. The lace-up boots stand small,
warm, like two sleeping hares, in the grass.

MUSIC OF THE FUTURE
ZUKUNFTSMUSIK

(1991)

Gillis van Coninxloo, Landschaft.
Holz, 64 x 119 cm

Die Verstoßung der Hagar,
scheußliche Scheidungsgeschichte,
Genesis 20, 21,
was daran heilig sein soll,
weiß der Himmel.

Aber der Faltenwurf,
aber das Wasser,
das unter der Brücke schäumt,
die spielenden Hunde, die Burg
auf dem Fels in der Ferne,
die Frau in der roten Schürze,
die auf dem Wasen die Wäsche auslegt
zum Bleichen, und der Fischer
in seinem Bretterhaus am Teich,
winzig—es sieht ganz so aus,
als wäre er eingeschlafen,
wie die Eule hoch im Geäst.

Dort, wo ich bin,
angelt niemand, kein Reiher
kreischt, die blaue Burg
ist keine blaue Burg, der Kampf
im Zimmer wirft keine Falten.

Eine Prise Pulver, in Öl gelöst,
das ist alles, auf einem Brett.
Es ist nicht da, was ich sehe,
es fehlt. Ein Trug der Augen.
Ich will betrogen sein
und betrügen.
Was daran heilig sein soll,
weiß der Himmel.
Unter der Brücke schäumen,
frischer als Wasser,
Grünspan, Bleiweiß und Malachit.

Gillis van Conninxloo, Landscape.
Panel, 65 x 119 cm

Hagar repudiated,
Genesis 20, 21,
an abominable divorce story,
supposed to be sacred,
Heaven knows why.

But then the folds of the robe,
the water foaming
beneath the bridge,
the playful hounds, the castle
on the rock in the distance,
the woman with the red apron
spreading her linen to bleach
in the meadow, and in his shed
the fisherman by the pond,
a tiny figure—it seems
as if he had gone to sleep,
like the owl in the fork of the tree.

Here, at my place,
no one is fishing, no heron
will screech, the blueish castle
ceases to be a castle, the fight
in my room will cast no folds.

A pinch of powder dissolved in oil,
that is all, and spread on a board.
What I see is absent,
a *trompe-l'œil*. I ask
for deception,
I wish to deceive.
Art's supposed to be sacred,
Heaven knows why.
Beneath the bridge I see foaming
white lead, malachite, verdigris,
fresher than water.

Der Augenschein

Du sagst:
Ich mache die Augen auf und sehe was da ist
zum Beispiel dort an der Wand diese nackte Frau da
oder hier diesen öden Bleistift
oder das Auge das mich unaufhörlich anstarrt zum Verrücktwerden
Ich mache die Augen zu und sehe was nicht da ist

So einfach ist das
So leicht bist du zu täuschen

Denn in Wirklichkeit steht die Wirklichkeit Kopf
auch dein Kopf auch das Kino in deinem Kopf

Woher weißt du ob sich das Auge bewegt und das Bild steht still
oder das Auge steht still und das Bild bewegt sich?

Sicher ist nur daß das Verschwundene nicht verschwunden ist
und das Vorhandene nicht vorhanden

Entweder du siehst das Kino oder den Film
entweder das Auge oder das Bild

Und deshalb starrst du unaufhörlich diese nackte Frau an
die sich nicht bewegt
mit aufgerissenen Augen zum Verrücktwerden
diese Frau die nicht da ist
und blickst mit geschlossenen Augen auf diese öde Brille hier
auf dieses Massaker im Kino
auf diese Gegenstände die vor dir auf dem Tisch tanzen

So einfach ist das
So leicht bist du zu täuschen

Oder du blickst in ein paar Augen in denen sich deine Augen spiegeln
in denen sich ein Paar Augen spiegeln in die du blickst

Mach die Augen auf und das Erscheinende ist verschwunden
Mach die Augen zu und das Verschwundene erscheint

Appearances

You say:
I open my eyes and see what is there
for instance there on the wall this female nude
or this dreary pencil down here
or the eye that stares at me so incessantly, it could drive me mad
I close my eyes and see what is not there.

It's as simple as that
That easily you're deceived

For in reality reality stands on its head
and so does your head and the cinema in your head

How can you know whether the eye moves and the image stays fixed
Or the eye stays fixed and the image moves?

All that's sure is that the vanished thing has not vanished
and the present thing is not present

Either you see the cinema or the film
either the eye or the image

And that's why you stare incessantly at this female nude
who does not move
with eyes so wide-open, it could drive you mad
this woman who isn't there
and with your eyes closed look at this dreary pair of glasses
at this massacre on the screen
at these objects dancing in front of you on the table

It's as simple as that
That easily you're deceived

Or you look into a pair of eyes that mirror your eyes
that mirror a pair of eyes into which you look

Open your eyes and the thing that appeared has vanished
Close your eyes and the thing that vanished appears

Aber das siehst du nicht ein
Du sagst:
Ich mache die Augen auf und sehe was da ist

usw. ad infnitum

But you won't see that
You say:
I open my eyes and see what is there

etc. ad infinitum

Das leere Blatt

Das, was du jetzt in der Hand hältst, ist beinah weiß,
aber nicht ganz; etwas ganz Weißes gibt es nicht;
es ist glatt, hart, zäh, dünn, und für gewöhnlich
knistert es, fließt, knirscht, reißt, beinah geruchlos;
und so wie es ist, bleibt es nicht; es bedeckt sich
mit Lügen, saugt alle Schrecken auf, alle Widersprüche,
Träume, Ängste, Künste, Tränen, Begierden;
bis sie getrocknet sind, vergilbt, stockig, grau;
bis es aufweicht, im Regen, zerfällt, im Müll,
immer weniger wird; nur das beste vielleicht
—an dem vielleicht das, was keiner geschrieben hat,
das Beste ist: ein Fisch, ein Salzfaß, ein Stern,
ein Einhorn, ein Elefant oder ein Ochsenkopf,
Zeichen des Heiligen Lukas; das, was erscheint,
wenn du es gegen das Licht hältst—hält,
vielleicht, tausend Jahre, oder noch eine Minute.

The Blank Sheet

What you're holding now in your hand is almost white,
but not quite; there is no such thing as a pure white thing;
it is smooth, hard, tough, thin and usually
it rustles, flows, crackles, tears, almost odourless;
and does not remain what it is; it covers itself
with lies, absorbs all the horrors, contradictions,
dreams, anxieties, skills, tears, desires;
until they desiccate, yellowing, spotted, grey;
until it grows sodden, in rain, disintegrates, as rubbish,
becomes less and less; only the best perhaps—
of which that, perhaps, which no one has written
is best of all: a fish, a salt cellar, star,
a unicorn, an elephant or an ox head,
the emblem of St Luke; that which appears
when you hold it against the light—lasts
a thousand years, perhaps, or another minute.

Konsistenz

Der Gedanke
hinter den Gedanken.
Ein Kiesel, gewöhnlich,
unvermischt, hart,
nicht zu verkaufen.

Löst sich nicht auf,
steht nicht
zur Diskussion,
ist was er ist,
nimmt nicht zu oder ab.

Unregelmäßig,
nicht bunt, geädert.
Nicht neu, nicht alt.
Braucht keine Begründung,
verlangt keinen Glauben.

Du weißt nicht, woher
du ihn hast, wohin
er geht, wozu
er dient. Ohne ihn
wärst du wenig.

Consistency

The thought
behind the thought.
A pebble, ordinary,
homogeneous, hard,
not for sale.

Does not dissolve,
is not
debatable,
is what it is,
does not gain or lose weight.

Irregular,
not brightly coloured, not veined.
Not new, not old.
Needs no substantiation,
demands no belief.

You don't know where
you get it from, where
it's going, what purpose
it serves. Without it
you wouldn't be much.

Alte Revolution

Ein Käfer, der auf dem Rücken liegt.
Die alten Blutflecken sind noch da, im Museum.
Jahrzehnte, die sich totstellen.
Ein saurer Mundgeruch dringt aus dreißig Ministerien.
Im Hotel Nacional spielen vier verstorbene Musikanten
den Tango von 1959, Abend für Abend:
Quizás, quizás, quizás.

Im Gemurmel der tropischen Maiandacht
fallen der Geschichte die Augen zu.
Nur die Sehnsucht nach Zahnpasta,
Glühbirnen und Spaghetti
liegt schlaflos da zwischen feuchten Laken.

Ein Somnambule vor zehn Mikrophonen,
der kein Ende findet, schärft seiner müden Insel ein:
Nach mir kommt nichts mehr.
Es ist erreicht.
An den Maschinenpistolen glänzt das Öl.
Der Zucker klebt in den Hemden.
Die Prostata tut es nicht mehr.

Sehnsüchtig sucht der greise Krieger
den Horizont ab nach einem Angreifer.
Aber die Kimm ist leer. Auch der Feind
hat ihn vergessen.

Old Revolution

A beetle lying on its back.
The old bloodspots are still on show
in the museum. Decades playing dead.
A sour smell from the mouth of thirty ministries.
At the Hotel Nacional four deceased musicians
are playing night by night the tango from '59:
Quizás, quizás, quizás.

By the murmur of a tropical rosary
History is taking a nap. Only those
who long for toothpaste, light bulbs
and spaghetti are tossing sleeplessly
between the damp bedsheets.

A sleepwalker in front of ten microphones
is preaching to his tired island:
After me nothing will follow.
It is finished.
The machine-guns glisten with oil.
The shirts are sticky with cane-juice.
The prostate has had it.

Wistfully the aged warrior
scans the horizon for an aggressor.
There is no one in sight. Even the enemy
has forgotten about him.

Restlicht

Doch doch, ich gehöre auch zu denen,
die es hier aushalten. Leicht sogar,
im Vergleich zu Kattowitz oder Montevideo.
Hie und da Reste von Landschaft,
rostende Eisenbahnschienen, Hummeln.
Ein kleiner Fluß, Erlen und Haselnüsse,
weil das Geld nicht gereicht hat
zur Begradigung. Über dem trüben Wasser
das Summen der Hochspannungsmasten
stört mich nicht. Es redet mir ein,
daß ich noch eine Weile lang
lesen könnte, bevor es dunkel wird.
Und wenn ich mich langweilen will,
ist das Fernsehen da, der farbige Wattebausch
auf den Augen, während draußen
die kindlichen Selbstmörder auf ihren Hondas
um den nassen Platz heulen. Auch der Krach,
auch die Rachsucht ist noch ein Lebenszeichen.
Im halben Licht vor dem Einschlafen
keine Kolik, kein wahrer Schmerz.
Wie einen leichten Muskelkater
spüren wir gähnend, sie und ich,
die von Minute zu Minute
kleiner werdende Zeit.

Residual Light

Oh yes, I, too, am one of those
who can stand it here. Easily, I would say,
compared to Katowice or Montevideo.
There are bits of landscape left
if you look for them, rusty rails,
humble-bees, alder and hazelnut on the bank
of a river spared by the engineers
for lack of development funds. I do not mind
the hum of the high-tension wires
above the murky waters. They would have me believe
that I could read for a while
before the lights go out.
And if I want to be bored,
there is the TV's colourful cotton wad
for the eyes, while outside
infantile suicides are circling the wet square
on their howling Hondas. Even the noise,
the resentment are signs of life.
In the half-light before I go to sleep
I feel no colic, no real pain.

Verschwundene Arbeit

Ziemlich entlegen, das alles.
Dunkel wie eine Sage.
Der Lumpenhändler
mit dem zerbeulten Zylinder,
des Waidmüllers blaue Hand,
der Pfragner in seinem kühlen Gewölb.

Der Schlözer stieg aus dem Schilf,
es ließ der Zedler die Beute stehn,
der Kohler den Quandel.
Die Kremplerin warf die Distel hin,
der Mollenhauer den Beitel.
Vermoderte Werke,
ausgestorbene Fertigkeiten.

Wo ist der Blatthaken geblieben,
die Zugöse, der Kammdeckel?
Verschollen der Schirrmacher,
nur der Name steht noch,
wie in Bernstein erstarrt,
im Telefonbuch.

Aber den schimmernden Quader aus Licht
habe ich selbst noch gesehen,
mit eigenen Augen, zauberhaft
mühelos in die Höhe geworfen
am eisernen Haken
auf das lederne Schulterblatt

des Eismanns, am Mittwoch,
pünktlich, die Splitter
schmolzen mir feurig
im kalten Mund.

Vanished Work

Rather remote, all of it.
As in a saga, darkly,
the rag-and-bone-man
with his battered top hat,
the blue hand of the woad-miller,
the corn-chandler in his cool cellar.

The rush-man has deserted his reed,
the beekeeper his hive,
the charcoal burner his flue.
The woolcarder threw her teasel away,
the trough-maker his chisel.
Trades mouldered away,
extinct skills.

What has happened to the bridoons,
the hames and the terrets?
The cartwright has passed away.
Only his name survives,
like an insect congealed in amber,
in the telephone book.

But the shimmering block of light
I have lived to see
with my own eyes, heaved
easily, as if by magic
with an iron hook
onto the leathery shoulder-strap

of the iceman, on Wednesdays
at noon, punctually, and the chips
melted like fire
in my chill mouth.

Der Eisenwarenladen

Zwei ältliche Waisen,
die ihn geerbt haben,
neunzehnjährig,
vor neunzehn Jahren.

Nonnen in verwaschenen Schürzen,
eingemauert
von bleiernen Schubladen,
Stifte und Stellschrauben
zwischen den Lippen.

Ihr grauer Eifer,
ihre rosige Hingabe
unter der nackten Glühbirne.
Der graue Geruch nach Schmierfett,
Gummi, Kitt und Metall.

Riesige Rohrzangen, Herzbohrer
in ungeliebten Händen.
Die feuchte Zunge,
die sich nach dem Mundwinkel sehnt
beim Schreiben der Rechnung.

Ursuppe, hast du dir davon
etwas träumen lassen?
Was hast du dir, Weltgeist,
dabei gedacht?
Vorsehung, war das alles:

Zwei ältliche Schwestern,
lebenslänglich,
in einem Eisenwarenladen?
Ihr rosiger Eifer,
ihre graue Hingabe
an das Schmirgelpapier?

The Ironmonger's Shop

Two elderly orphans
who inherited it
when they were nineteen,
nineteen years ago.

Nuns in washed-out aprons,
walled in by leaden chests
of drawers,
tacks and adjusting screws
between their lips.

Their rosy devotion,
their greying eagerness
under the naked light bulb,
the grey smell of grease,
of rubber, metal and putty.

Enormous wrenches, breast drills
in unloved hands.
The moist tongue
longing for another mouth
while the bill is made out.

Is this what you dreamt of,
Primal Soup? *Weltgeist*,
did you have your wits about you?
Was that all you had in mind,
Divine Providence?

Two elderly sisters
imprisoned for life
in an ironmonger's shop?
Their rosy eagerness,
their grey devotion
to the emery-paper?

Alte Ehepaare

Wer so lange geblieben ist,
macht sich wenig vor.

»Ich weiß, daß ich nichts weiß«:
Auch das ist noch übertrieben.

Alte Ehepaare
haben nichts übrig
für das Überflüssige,
lassen das Unentscheidbare
in der Schwebe.

Merkwürdig distanziert,
dieser luzide Blick.
Kühne Rückzüge,
geplant
von langer Hand.

Andrerseits hartnäckig
wie der Schachtelhalm.
Resignation—
ein Fremdwort.

Improvisierte Krücken,
Selbsthilfe, Kartoffeln
im eigenen Garten
und im Zweifelsfall,
am Kreuzweg,
die Sauerstoffmaske zur Hand.

Man sieht manches,
wenn das Licht ausgeht.

Old Couples

Those who have stayed so long
don't kid themselves much.

'I know that I know nothing':
even that would be an exaggeration.

Old married couples
have no use for overstatements;
they leave open
what cannot be settled.

Their glance is lucid
and strangely distant.
Bold retreats,
planned
long in advance.

On the other hand
they are dogged like marestail.
Resignation
is Greek to them.

Improvised crutches,
self-help, homegrown potatoes,
and if the worst,
comes to the worst,
at the crossroads,
the oxygen mask at hand.

There is much to be seen
when the lights go out.

Valse triste et sentimentale

Ja, früher, früher!
Und was ist jetzt?
Mach was du willst,
aber sei so lieb:
Keine Rechtfertigungen.

Mit oder ohne,
du hast jedenfalls.
Beziehungsweise
du hast nicht.
Das genügt.

»Was soll ich *denn* machen?
Was soll ich *denn* machen?«
Natürlich. Das kennt man.
Das fragen sie immer,
wenn es zu spät ist.

Eigentlich schade.
Manchmal vermiß ich dich schon
mit deinen ewigen Dramen,
deinen blöden Ausreden,
deinem faulen Zauber.

Ich, schlechtes Gewissen?
Da kann ich nur lachen.
Mach die Tür zu
und laß dich nie wieder
blicken!

Valse triste et sentimentale

Blast the old days.
What about now?
Do as you like,
but please,
no apologies.

You did, didn't you?
With or without it.
Or else
you didn't.
That's all there is to it.

'What do you want me to do?
What do you want me to do?'
Of course. I know.
That's what they all ask
when it's too late.

A pity, really.
Sometimes I begin to miss you
with your eternal scenes,
your foggy excuses,
your hocus pocus.

Me, feeling guilty?
You make me laugh.
Get out of here
and don't show your face again,
ever.

Fetisch

Immer nur
an diesen Flaum
denkt er nachts
kleiner
als eine Hand
und weiter
denkt er
an nichts
Nichts anderes
ist da
als dieses Büschel
das nicht da ist
Er stellt es sich
dunkel vor
dieses Gewölle
wie es sich bauscht
hell
Er hört förmlich
wie es knistert
unter dem Druck
der Hand
Er sieht
wie es sich kräuselt
im Licht
blond schwarz
wie es glitzert
wahnsinnig
weich und widerspenstig
und nicht weiter
nennenswert

Fetish

All night
he is thinking of it
a wisp of down
smaller
than the hand of a man
There is nothing else
he can think of
there is nothing
but this tuft of hair
which is not here
He imagines it
dark
a woolly mass
curling
brightly
He can almost hear it
rustle
at the touch of his hand
He sees it
bristling
in the light
blonde black
soft and unruly
glittering madly
and scarcely worth
further notice

Schlaftablette

Bunte Raumkapsel
winziges Senfkorn der Amnesie
das seinen Kern entblößt
in der Neige der Sintflut

Weißer Taifun im Wasserglas
chemischer Katarakt
den ich austrinke
der mich ertränkt

Schlieriges *chiaroscuro*
Blauer Nil
der mein Gehirn marmoriert
bis ich untergetaucht bin

Stilles Mirakel
aus zentnerschweren Milligrammen
in dem ich meine Angst aus-
hauche und meine Freude

bis tief in den schrillen Tag

Sleeping Pill

Gaudy space capsule
tiny mustard seed of amnesia
revealing its core
in the lees of the deluge

White typhoon in a glass of water
chemical cataract
which I drain
in which I drown

Cloudy *chiaroscuro*
Blue Nile
marbling my brain
until I am submerged

Mute miracle bearing down
grain by grain like a hundredweight
You help me to breathe my last worry
and my last joy

until the next shrill noon

Zum Ewigen Frieden

Dieses Zeug, das aus dem dunklen
Himmel hell fällt, leicht,
gleichmäßig, lautlos, ohne
Aufenthalt tänzelnd, setzt sich

auf alles, ohne Eile, was eckig
ist, Hochhaus, Briefkasten, Sarg.
Alles, was eckig war, wird
rund, langsam bauschen sich

Mauern, der Abdruck der Schuhe
füllt sich, geht unter, mild,
es versinkt die Schaufel,
langsam, langsam, alles, was

zählbar war, spitz, distinkt,
fließt ineinander, Dachziegel,
Köpfe, behaubt sich, es unterliegt
das Schroffe dem Weichen, es weicht

der Unterschied, niedrig, hoch,
flach, erhaben, böse, gut. Da
der Hügel war vor Wochen, Tagen,
Minuten ein Puff, eine Bretterbude,

ein Schneepflug. Auch die Zeit
ist zu Watte geworden. Hie und da
noch ein Wetterhahn, eine Antenne.
Die leichte Wölbung am Horizont

undeutlich, von Flocken verschluckt,
muß das Matterhorn sein, oder
der Ararat. Es verschwindet der Krieg
im Frieden, weiß und vollkommen.

Alles gleichmäßig wie der Schnee,
nur der Schnee nicht. Jeder Kristall
für sich, verschieden von

Towards Eternal Peace

All this light stuff falling down
from the dark sky brightly,
prancing without respite,
without a sound, evenly

squatting, without haste,
on all things square,
building coffin letterbox.
All things square bulge

slowly, walls billow, footprints
fill up and are erased,
mildly, the shovel sinks
into oblivion, slowly, slowly,

all things countable,
sharp, distinct, merge
and become submerged, heads
and roofs are hooded, rigour

gives way to softness, differences
dwindle: low, high, uneven, flat,
good, evil. Weeks, days, minutes ago
the hill over there was a booth,

a brothel, a snow-plow. Time, too,
has turned into cotton wool.
Goodbye to the weather-cock, the antenna.
That slight bulge in the horizon,

embalmed by flakes, shrouded
in vagueness, must be the Matterhorn,
or Mount Ararat. War dissolves
into peace, white and perfect.

All things even out in the snow,
except the snow. Each crystal
is on its own, differing

jedem Kristall. Ein Blick
durch das Mikroskop genügt, nur
schade, daß es versunken ist,
das Mikroskop, und das Auge
verdunkelt vom Schnee.

from the next, as a glance
through the microscope would show.
A pity that it has gone under,
our microscope, and the eye
is blacked out by the snow.

Ein Hase im Rechenzentrum

Die schnellste Maschine,
Parallelarchitektur,
knapp tausend Megaflops,
vermag seinem kleinen Gehirn
nicht zu folgen.

Die bebende Oberlippe
zuckend im Neonlicht,
die großen Augen starr
auf den Bildschirm gerichtet,
trommelt er panisch
gegen das graue Linoleum.

Dann, es ist drei Uhr früh,
der letzte Plasmaphysiker
ist nach Hause gegangen,
schnellt er plötzlich hoch
und jagt im Zickzack
zwischen Monitoren
und stotternden Druckern
durch den verlassenen Raum.

Weicher Feigling,
fünfzig Millionen Jahre
älter als wir!
Dem Blutdurst der Jäger,
der Ramme, dem Gas,
dem Virus entkommen,
schlägt er ungerührt seine Haken.

Aus dem Eozän hoppelt er
an uns vorbei in eine Zukunft,
reich an Feinden,
doch nahrhaft und geil
wie der Löwenzahn.

A Hare in the Data Processing Centre

The fastest of our machines,
parallel architecture,
close to a thousand megaflops,
cannot keep up
with its miniscule brain.

Its upper lip in a quiver
it twitches in the neon glare,
the large eyes staring fixedly
at the monitor screen,
it panics, its hindleg drumming
against the grey lino floor.

Past three o'clock in the morning,
when the last plasma physicist
has gone home, it suddenly jumps
and zigzags in a wild chase
past work stations
and stuttering printers
through the deserted hall.

Soft coward,
fifty million years
older than we are!
Having survived
rammer, poison gas, virus,
it goes on intrepidly
doubling the hunters.

Out of the eocene
it hobbles past us into a future
rich in enemies
but nourishing and rank
like dandelion.

Limbisches System

Es ist alt, es ist weich,
es versteht sich nicht,
weiß nicht, was *limbus* bedeutet,
was ein System ist

Zwischen Gewölbe und Balken
eine Vorhölle, winzig.

Ammonshorn, Gürtel, Mandelkern:
ein dunkles Gedächtnis,
das sich seiner selbst
nicht erinnern kann.

Unkontrollierbar
kontrolliert es
Angst Lust Mord Sucht

Seine Schleifen und Fasern
ein Kabelbaum
tief im Schädel,
intra- und extramural.

Kriechströme, Schwelbrände,
Kurzschlüsse.
Kleine Defekte,
die rasch eskalieren.

Ein Ruck in der Steuerung,
und es nimmt Rache.
Ein elektrischer Stoß,
und es läuft Amok.

Ein paar Milliarden Zellen
im Dunkeln. Das Menschengeschlecht,
ein winziges Knäuel
zwischen Anfang und Amnesie.

Limbic System

It is ancient, it is spongy,
does not understand itself,
has no idea what *limbus* means,
what a system is.

Between fornix and corpus callosum
a minuscule limbo.

Ammon's horn, belt, amygdala:
a dark memory
unable to recall itself.

It controls
fear lust murder addiction,
and no one controls it.

Its loops and fibres
pass through a cable duct
intra- and extra-murally
hidden in the depth of the skull.

Prone to leakage currents,
cable burnouts, short circuits.
Small faults
which escalate quickly.

An excessive input
and hell will break loose.
An electric shock
and it will run amuck.

A few billion cells in the dark.
Man manhandled
by a lump in the brain
between birth and amnesia.

Das Gift

Nicht, wie es früher war, rund,
wenig, ein Gran, verschlossen
wie eine Beere, wie eine Erbse
klein, verborgen in einem Ring,
einer Kapsel, privat, minimal,
heimlich wie eine fixe Idee,

sondern offenbar wie ein Meer,
schwerwiegend und normal,
breit verteilt, wie der Wind
entfesselt, wolkig, geruchlos
und ebensowenig zu fassen, all-
gegenwärtig wie früher Gott,

der, ein privates Gran,
wenig, immer weniger wiegt,
wie eine Erbse, heimlich,
wie eine Tollkirsche
in der Brust, verschlossen
wie eine fixe Idee.

The Poison

Not, as it used to be, round,
little, a grain, sealed
like a berry, a pea,
tiny, concealed in a ring,
a capsule, private, minimal,
secret like an *idée fixe*,

but manifest like the sea,
ponderous and normal,
widely distributed, like the wind
unleashed, cloudy, odourless
and as impalpable, omni-
present as God was once

who, a private grain,
little, weighs less and less,
like a pea, secret,
like a deadly nightshade seed
in one's breast, sealed
like an *idée fixe*.

Vorgänger

Abgewandt, früher
oder später, abgewandt
haben sie sich,
einer nach dem andern.
Zuerst die Augen,
unmerklich, dann
diese minimale Geste
der linken Hand,
die zu deuten
uns nicht gegeben war.

Ein Abwinken,
ein ironischer Gruß:
»Wir stellen anheim,
lassen auf sich beruhn.«
Aber was?

Erst, als wir
das glatte Kissen fanden,
die leere Tasse,
das Hemd über dem Stuhl,
den Schlüssel am Brett,
waren wir irritiert.

»Was hast du?«
Keine Antwort.
Weder Vorwurf
noch Nachsicht.
Nicht einmal das Licht
haben sie ausgemacht
im Korridor.

Dann sind sie
kleiner geworden,
immer kleiner,
wie Flugzeuge, oder
wenn sie zu Fuß waren,
im Schnee, dunkel,

Precursors

Turned away, sooner
or later, they have
turned away,
one after the other.
First the eyes,
imperceptibly, then
this minimal gesture
of the left hand
which to construe
was beyond our gift.

A waving aside,
an ironic greeting:
'We leave it open,
we let the matter rest.'
But what?

Only when we
found the smooth cushion,
the empty cup,
the shirt across the chair,
the key hung up,
we were annoyed.

'What's biting you?'
No answer.
Neither reproach
nor consideration.
They didn't even
switch off the light
in the corridor.

Then they grew smaller,
smaller and smaller
like aircraft, or
when they walked,
in snow, dark,

auf Knüppeldämmen,
in einer Staubwolke.

Was aus ihnen geworden ist,
wissen wir nicht.

on log roads,
in a cloud of dust.

What's become of them
we do not know.

Abtrift

Das Gehirn im Sinkflug,
immer tiefer.
An den Spanndrähten
zerrt der Abwind.
Das Steuer flattert,
schlägt aus,
»von selbst«.
Auch eine Musik:
rauschende Luft,
knirschendes Holz.
Es knackt im Holm,
im Ohr, im Kopf.
Schmerzloser Sog,
selbstvergessen,
feierlich leichtes
Gleiten, dem
Dunkleren zu.

Leeway

The brain on its descent,
lower and lower.
Against the tension wires
the down-draught tugs.
The rudder flutters,
veers
'by itself'.
A music too:
rushing air,
creaking timbers.
There's a crack in the spar,
in the ear, in the head.
Painless suction,
self-oblivious,
solemnly weightless
gliding towards
the darker place.

Seltsamer Attraktor

Minuten-, stunden-, tagelang
gebeugt über das Geländer.
über Millionen
von unlösbaren Gleichungen,
seh ich ins Aug des Zyklons,
der mir ins Auge sieht;

kalkgrün, weißschäumend
rauscht die helle Materie,
hypnotisch kreisend,
die glitzernde Gischt,
in wiederkehrenden Strudeln
nie wiederkehrend;

und obenauf, flaumig,
im Schaum, im Licht,
taumelt, tanzt etwas Nasses,
Braunes, das tanzt,
aber nicht untergeht,
taumelt ein Teddybär.

Strange Attractor

Bent over the railing
for minutes hours days,
over millions of equations
with no solution in sight,
I look into the eye of a cyclone
that looks me straight in the eye;

chalky green, foamy white
live matter roaring on
in hypnotic swirls,
turning in bright eddies
and glittering cycles
which never recur;

and on top of the foam,
wet, brown and downy,
bobbing up and down,
rolling dizzily in the light
but not going under,
tumbles a teddy bear.

KIOSK

KIOSK
(1997)

Asphodelen

Komisch, der Gnostiker
im vierten Stock
ist immer noch wach.
Er klopft und klopft
an das Heizungsrohr.
Vor dem Fenster der Mob
ist verschwunden, und jetzt
fängt es auch noch zu schneien an.

In der ganzen Stadt
gibt es keine Schnürsenkel mehr.
Das MG-Feuer im Bankenviertel
hat nachgelassen.
Aber es sind noch ein paar
Asphodelen da, im Kühlschrank,
für all Fälle.

Asphodels

Odd—the Gnostic
on the fourth floor
is still awake.
He bangs and bangs
against the radiator.
The mob at the window
has disappeared, and now,
on top of it all, it's beginning to snow.

The entire city
is out of shoelaces.
The machine-gun fire in the financial district
has died down.
But there are still a few
asphodels left, in the fridge,
just in case.

Gedankenflucht (I)

Als wäre gleich hinter Helsinki
oder Las Palmas alles ganz anders,
überall Umzüge, Fluchtgedanken.
Ganze Ortschaften kommen abhanden.

Im Flutlicht, hinter Absperrungen,
die Spastiker der Macht
über Karten gebeugt. Dann
ein neuer Schlagfluß der Geschichte,
und es geht wieder los.

Jahrzehntelang gestauchter Haß.
Absichten zählen kaum.
Noch mehr Nomaden
taumeln über die Straßen.

Was nicht nötig ist, das Meiste,
bleibt zurück, Sperrmüll,
Nähmaschinen, Gesammelte Werke.

Auch du, mein Alter, läßt dich bewegen,
bewegst dich. Bei aller Liebe.
Wozu? Was suchst du? Dollars,
Maniok, Spaß, Munition?
Oder nur deine Ruhe?
»Ich suche eine Erklärung.«

Der kann von Glück sagen, der nur
wie du auf der Autobahn
ins Schleudern gerät: Mull
ist immer da, Blaulicht auch.

Anderswo heißt es: Die letzte Maschine
aus Juba, Lubango, Phnom Penh
ist soeben gelandet. Babyflaschen,
Bettzeug, geplatzte Koffer—
Ende der Durchsage.

Thoughts on the Run I

As if just beyond Helsinki
or Las Palmas everything were totally different,
everywhere relocations, thoughts of escape.
Whole municipalities get lost.

Under floodlights, behind barricades,
the spastics of power
bent over maps. Then
a new hemorrhage of history,
and it starts over again.

Decades of bottled-up hate.
Intentions hardly matter.
Still more vagabonds
stagger across the streets.

What's unnecessary, most of it,
stays behind, old armchairs,
sewing machines, Collected Works.

You, too, pal, can be moved,
do move. For chrissakes.
Why? What are you looking for? Dollars,
cassava, fun, ammunition?
Or just peace and quiet?
"I'm looking for an explanation."

He can count himself lucky
who, like you, only happens to skid
on the freeway: gauze
is always around, and sirens.

Somewhere else it is said: The last plane
from Yuba City, Lubango, Phnom Penh
has just landed. Baby bottles,
bed sheets, busted suitcases—
end of announcement.

Etwas Zerfetztes im Minenfeld,
daneben ein unverwundeter Schuh,
Flöße in der Karibik,
alles kommt über Satellit,
wird gespeichert d.h. vergessen.

Traumurlaub oder Panik,
jedenfalls Pulks, Karawanen,
Stau, Mangel an Überblick,
stop and go, Herzklopfen,
hier und da ein Hubschrauber,
und vor dir die Bremslichter
deiner Vorfahren, eine Kette
von roten Punkten im Smog.

Auch dieser Krieg
ist noch nicht zu Ende.

Something shredded in the mine field,
nearby an uninjured shoe,
rafts in the Caribbean,
everything's carried by satellite,
will be stored, i.e. forgotten.

Dream vacation or panic,
in any case crowds of cars, caravans,
congestion, low visibility,
stop and go, heart palpitations,
a helicopter here and there,
and in front of you the brake lights
of your ancestors, a chain
of red dots in the smog.

This war's not
over yet, either.

Gedankenflucht (II)

Etwas, woran du dich halten kannst—
warum nicht? Paßnummer,
Arbeitsplatz, »amtliche Offenbarung«.
Allerdings, lebenslänglich
ist auch keine Lösung.
Optimismus: ein Münchhausen-Problem.

Bewegst du dich,
oder wirst du bewegt?
Umwege, schlingernde Bahnen
im Phasenraum der Gefühle.

Der Alte kannst du nicht bleiben,
nicht allda, bei der Stange,
auch bei der Sache nicht
(welcher Sache?).
Das mußt du bleiben lassen.

Aber was dann? Ein Dach, ein Wort,
ein Versteck, einen Rückweg,
oder, wenn es dunkel wird,
wenigstens eine Matte—
das suchen alle.

Eigentümlich porös,
deine Fluchtgedanken.
Sie lieben, kämpfen, falten,
vermischen sich, triebhaft.
Du bist ein Mestize.

(Blauschwarz, rosa, oliv—
damals, in Lima, haben die Sieger
mehr als zwanzig Farben unterschieden,
Halb-, Viertel-, Achtelblütige,
zambigos, zambopretos,
zamboclaros und saltatrás.)

Thoughts on the Run II

Something you can hold on to—
why not? Passport number,
workplace, "official statement."
Well, a life sentence's
no solution, either.
Optimism: a problem á la Münchhausen.

Do you move,
or are you moved?
Detours, veering channels
in the transitional space of feelings.

You can't remain who you were,
sticking to your guns
lock, stock, and barrel
(what guns?).
You have to let it go.

But then what? A roof, a word,
a hideaway, a way back,
or, when it grows dark,
at least a pallet—
everybody looks for that.

Oddly porous,
your thoughts of escape.
They love, fight, fold over
each other, mix carnally.
You are a mestizo.

(Blueblack, pink, olive—
back then, in Lima, the conquerors
specified more than twenty colors,
half-, quarter-, and one eighth-blooded,
zambigos, zambopretos,
zamboclaros and *saltatrás*.)

Zusammengewürfelt in Betten,
auf Schlachtfeldern. »Das Leben«—
ein gleichgewichtsferner Oszillator.
Absichten zählen kaum.

Unter uns bleiben wir nicht.
Es bleibt nicht beim Alten.
Dabei bleibt es. Alles weitere
bleibt abzuwarten.

Thrown together in beds,
on battlefields. "Life"—
an oscillator far from equilibrium.
Intentions hardly matter.

We don't keep to ourselves.
Nothing stops where it was.
So it goes. Everything else
remains to be seen.

Gedankenflucht (III)

Daß es nicht dabei bleibt,
gilt auch für die Steine.
Das Gebirge dehnt sich, fleißt,
pulsiert, rauscht, reißt,
wenn auch langsam.
Was heißt schon langsam
bei einem Berg?

Energien unter der Erdkruste,
unter der Hirnschale. Siehst du,
wie sich das alles bewegt,
vermischt, faltet, dehnt,
auch das, was du nicht siehst?

»Der Begriff der Totalität
existiert in der Theorie,
nicht im Leben.«
Unter uns, in den Gräbern
sammelt sich manches an.

Auch die Wissenschaft ist porös,
atmet schwer, huscht panisch
durch ihre Anstalt; auch er,
der Biologe, lernfähig und verirrt
wie sein Meerschwein, sucht,
bis er, selten genug, ach,
die erlösende Taste drückt.

Dann eine kurze Erleuchtung,
eine Ausschüttung von Glück,
flackernd, auf dem Weg
zu neuen Verfinsterungen.

Ja, besuche sie nur, die Deponien
im Norden der Stadt,
wühle darin, Augur,
abgefallener Theologe
des Abfalls!

Thoughts on the Run III

That it doesn't stop there
is also true for the stones.
The mountains expand, flow,
pulse, roar, split,
although slowly.
But what does slow mean
to a mountain?

Energy under the earth's crust,
under the cranium. Can you see
how all of it is moving,
mixing, folding, expanding,
even what you don't see?

"The concept of totality
exists in theory,
not in life."
Just between us, there's a lot
accumulating in the graves.

Science is also porous,
breathes with difficulty, scurries panicked
through its institution; even
the biologist, trainable and confused
like his guinea pig, searches
until he presses—so seldom!—
the triggering key.

Then a brief enlightenment,
an outpouring of luck,
flickering en route
to fresh gloominess.

Sure, go visit the dumps
north of the city,
rummage around, Augur,
lapsed theologian
of garbage!

Ein betäubender Duft.
Vieles natürlich giftig,
wie die Natur, wie du und ich:
mutierte Samen, Wucherndes, Viren—
du merkst es den Blättern an,
die Flecken zeigen, ein Mosaik
von Verfärbungen,
rosa, blauschwarz, oliv,
Abweichungen, unberechenbar
wie die Bahnen am Himmel.

Vielschichtig schwelen die Freuden.
Alles Besinnungslose
sammelt sich hier, beschildert.
Ja, auch Vorschriften gibt es,
Warnungen. Ach, du tust dein Bestes,
was ist das schon—
Absichten zählen kaum.

Du ziehst um, fliehst,
vermischst dich mit dem,
was der Fall ist.

Auf Weiterungen
heißt es gefaßt sein.
Bei uns bleibt es nicht.

A bewitching aroma.
Much of it poisonous, of course,
like Nature, like you and I:
mutant seeds, proliferations, viruses—
you can tell by the leaves,
which show spots, a mosaic
or discolorations,
pink, blueblack, olive,
variations unpredictable
as jet trails in the sky.

Pleasures smolder on many levels.
All that's unconscious
collects here, labeled.
Yes, there are also regulations,
warnings. Ah, you do your best,
but so what—
intentions hardly matter.

You move away, flee,
get mixed in with
whatever's up.

Brace yourself
for further developments.
It won't stop with us.

Gedankenflucht (IV)

Die kleine Pilgerin da
auf ihrer chaotischen Bahn,
dieses umherirrende,
glimmende Nichts—
wie war doch der Name gleich?—
und was sucht sie nur,
die bis auf weiteres
unsterbliche Seele?

Sie wühlt im Müll,
unermüdlich, nach Weisheiten,
die plötzlich weg waren,
zerkrümelt in endlosen Permutationen,
vermoderten Paperbacks.

Sie kann nicht stillhalten,
will es nicht einsehen,
kann es einfach nicht fassen,
die winzige Wallfahrerin.

Wie sie sich faltet, dehnt,
faltet wie Blätterteig,
gewalkt von Energien
aus der Heliosphäre
und aus den tieferen Schichten
ihres Gehirns! Nein,

sie kann es nicht lassen,
vermischt sich, triebhaft,
nach alter Gewohnheit,
mit Wolken, Meeren, Gestirnen.

Bei dem, was der Fall ist,
bleibt es nicht. Ja,
sagt sie, ich will zurück,
ich will weiter, unabsehbar
bewege ich mich, bin bewegt,
bis auf weiteres bleibe ich,
in der Schwebe.

Thoughts on the Run IV

The little pilgrim there
on her chaotic path,
this errant,
glimmering nothing—
what exactly was her name?—
and what's she looking for,
the soul, immortal for the time being?

She rummages through garbage,
inexhaustible, looking for scraps of wisdom
that had suddenly vanished,
crumpled in endless permutations,
mildewed paperbacks.

She cannot keep still,
will not be reasonable,
simply doesn't get it,
the tiny wayfarer.

How she folds up, stretches,
folds like puff pastry,
battered by energies
from the heliosphere
and the deeper layers
of her brain! No,

she can't leave it alone,
this old habit,
and couples feverishly
with clouds, oceans, stars.

No matter what's up,
it doesn't stop there. Yes,
she says, I want to go back,
I want to go on, I move
unforseeably, am moved,
for the time being hang
in the balance.